דרך ה'

God and His Ways

To Understand the Supernal Reality of God

Ramchal
Rabbi Moshe Chaim Luzzatto

Translated by
Rav Raphael Afilalo

Hazohar555@gmail.com

kabbalah5.com - zoharvideos.com – ramchal.com

YouTube : Rav Raphael Afilalo – Zohar - Kabbalah

ISBN: 9782923241937

Publications by Rav Raphael Afilalo

English

Concepts of Kabbalah
Kabbalah Dictionary
Glossary of Kabbalah
Arizal Prince of the
Kabbalists
160 Questions on the
Kabbalah
Kabbalah of the Arizal,
according to the Ramhal
Gates of Reincarnations

French

Concepts de Kabbalah
Dictionnaire de Kabbalah
Glossaire de Kabbalah
Arizal Prince des
Kabbalistes
160 Questions sur la
Kabbalah
Kabbalah du Arizal, selon
le Ramhal
Portes des Réincarnations

Translations of books of the Ramchal

God and His Ways
The Kabbalist and the
Philosopher
The Way of the Justs
The Wisdom of
Consciousness

Dieu et Ses Voies
Le Kabbaliste et le
Philosophe
La Voie des Justes
La Sagesse de la
Conscience

בעברית

מושגי חכמת הקבלה

חשיבות לימוד הזהר

אריז''ל נשיא המקובלים

קיצור כתבי האري

קבלה – תורה האמת

הזהר – כתבים מיסטיים של פנמיוה התורה

Translator's foreword

This important work by the Ramchal opens by elucidating the immense value and advantage of properly comprehending reality through methodically grasping the precise configuration and interrelation of its composite parts, rather than hastily viewing it as an undifferentiated, homogeneous whole without discernment of its internal structure. This orderly approach allows understanding things by carefully analyzing their composite elements and the connections between them.

For even if we conceptualizes the existence of many parts, without knowing the authentic connections and proper positioning of those component elements within the integrated structure, this leaves the yearning intellect burdened without satisfaction.

For one who properly discerns the precise nature and position of each constituent part according to its various aspects and relationships, the subject will unveil before him in its full integrated completeness. As the integrated comprehension is attained, the intellect will grasp the coherent beauty of its structured composition. The text elucidates the value of methodically analyzing reality's precise configuration rather than viewing it as a homogeneous whole. This orderly approach entails:

- Determining fundamental classifications (e.g. whole vs part)
- Discerning interrelations between elements
- Recognizing the absolute or bounded nature of things

- Grasping general principles encompassing details
- Tracing the progression of details.

The author systematically composed this work to facilitate comprehending the foundations of faith and divine service across four sections:

1. Foundations of Existence
2. Divine Providence
3. Prophecy
4. Proper Service

The goal is for the concepts to become absorbed within the reader, providing a basis for knowing God and Torah. This is why our Sages advise, "One should always have matters of Torah as general principles, not particular details." Yet general principles themselves must also be properly understood in the full scope of their rightful domain and aspects of applicability. For no detail or constituent element is truly negligible or inherently unworthy of concern, given that nothing exists entirely in isolation or without consequence at some level or context. The ultimate hope is that through this intellectual soul-journey, each word and concept contemplated will awaken within the sincere seeker enhanced vision, understanding and desire to walk amidst the wonders of Hashem's infinite wisdom, and in accordance with His compassionate ways.

The title "God and His Ways" reflects its focus on this most divine path.

Rav Raphael Afilalo

The life of the Ramchal

Moshe Chaim Luzzatto, known as the Ramchal, was an enigmatic figure in Jewish history, remembered as a philosopher, kabbalist, and poet whose works have had a lasting impact on Jewish thought and mysticism. Born in Padua, Italy, on April 26, 1707, into a distinguished family, Ramchal displayed prodigious intellectual capabilities from a young age.

His education was comprehensive, steeped in the dual worlds of Jewish and secular knowledge, which was a hallmark of the Italian Jewish renaissance. He was well-versed in the Torah, Talmud, and Kabbalistic literature, as well as the sciences and philosophy of his time, which informed his unique approach to Jewish theology and ethics.

The Ramchal's intellectual journey began with his study of the Talmud and other classic Jewish texts, but he was particularly drawn to the study of Kabbalah, the Jewish mystical tradition. By the age of 20, he had already begun writing his own commentaries on these subjects. His most famous work, "Mesillat Yesharim" (Path of the Just), is a systematic exploration of Jewish ethics and spiritual growth, which has become a foundational text in the Mussar movement, a Jewish ethical, educational, and cultural movement.

Despite his young age, the Ramchal's works, such as "Derech Hashem" (God and His Ways), which systematically presents the fundamentals of Jewish belief, demonstrated a mastery of

Jewish law and mysticism that few could rival. He also penned "Da'at Tevunot" (The Knowing Heart), a dialogue between the intellect and the soul on the nature of God's interaction with the world, and the purpose of Creation and human existence.

However, the Ramchal's intense involvement with Kabbalah, at a time when skepticism towards mysticism was widespread following the false messianic movement of Shabbetai Zvi, aroused suspicion. His formation of a select group of disciples to study Kabbalah led to further controversy. In 1727, under communal pressure in Italy, he agreed to a ban on teaching Kabbalah and ceased writing Kabbalistic works. This period of conflict was difficult for the Ramchal, whose only desire was to elevate the spiritual state of his people.

In search of a more accommodating environment for his Kabbalistic pursuits, Ramchal left Italy in 1735, eventually settling in Amsterdam. There, he hoped to live a life of spiritual and intellectual freedom. He supported himself by working as a diamond cutter and continued to write extensively. Amsterdam's Jewish community was a center of publishing, and it was there that he printed many of his works.

The Ramchal's life in Amsterdam allowed him some respite from the controversies that had followed him in Italy, and he continued his prolific writing, including works on Hebrew grammar and logic, such as "Sefer haHigayon" (The Book of Logic), which reflected his broader academic interests.

Despite his relatively comfortable life in Amsterdam, the Ramchal's longing for the Land of Israel was intense. In 1743, he and his family made the arduous journey to the Holy Land, settling in Acre. Tragically, his time there was short-lived; he died in a plague along with his family in 1746, at the young age of 39.

The Ramchal left behind a literary legacy that spans philosophical treatises, ethical texts, kabbalistic writings, poetry, plays, and more. His works continue to be studied for their depth and insight into the human condition and the divine.

Perhaps the most enduring aspect of the Ramchal's work is his ability to synthesize the mystical and rational aspects of Judaism. He believed that an understanding of the divine structure of the universe could lead to a profound religious life rooted in ethical conduct. His works have been embraced by various streams of Jewish thought, from the rationalist to the mystic, each finding in his writings a wellspring of knowledge and inspiration.

The legacy of the Ramchal is marked by a balance between the esoteric and the practical, the heavenly and the earthly. His vision of spiritual ascent is not one of withdrawal from the world but of engagement with it, guided by divine wisdom. His life and works serve as a bridge, inviting each person to traverse the gap between the finite and infinite, between human and divine potential.

The *Maggid* of Mezritch said:
"His generation did not merit this great man…. Many among our people, through lack of knowledge, have uttered on this saintly man calumny that was not justified."

The Gaon of Vilna declared that if Ramchal was still alive, he would have traveled to Italy on foot to learn from his wisdom.

Moshe Chaim Luzzatto's contributions to Jewish thought and his teachings are now universally recognized as treasures of Jewish literature, offering guidance to those who seek a path of righteousness, intellect, and spiritual introspection. The Ramchal remains a beacon of spiritual and moral guidance, whose influence continues to be felt centuries after his passing.

Introduction by the Ramchal

The sublime advantage of comprehending reality through grasping the precise configuration and interrelation of its constituent parts, rather than viewing it as an undifferentiated whole, is akin to the difference between observing an orderly garden beautifully arranged into beds, paths and rows, versus seeing a chaotic thicket or tangled forest. For though one may conceptualize many parts whose authentic connections and positioning within the integrated structure remains unknown, this leaves the intellect that yearns for true understanding burdened without satisfaction. Each element pictured in isolation excites curiosity about its completion within the whole, yet its deficient portrayal precludes this, thus troubling the mind and paining it with unquenched longing and unremitting confusion.

In dramatic contrast, one who properly discerns the nature of each part according to its various aspects beholds the subject unveiled before him in its fullness. The intellect then delights, following wherever interest leads within the beauty of its composition, as coherent comprehension is attained. For integral to properly understanding any topic is recognizing its essence and distinguishing parameters.

Thus, one must firstly determine the fundamental categorization and station of each element within the framework of reality. The primordial classifications are: whole or part; generality or particular; cause or effect; conveyer or addon. Correspondingly, initial analysis of any subject must establish whether it is a complete entity or constituent component; a universal principle or specific detail; an originating cause or resultant outcome; an underlying substrate or accrued attribute.

Profoundly, the precise aspects warranting examination stem from its innate properties and role. If part, one must identify the whole it helps comprise. If particular, its belonging generality is sought. Effects are traced to causes, and causes to antecedents. Adjuncts are scrutinized in light of their bearer. Additionally, the adjunct's nature is examined - whether preceding, following or concomitant; whether essential or happenstantial; potential or extant; etc. For absent such methodical distinctions, no well-formed conceptualization is possible.

Most crucially, the absolute or delimited nature of each matter must be determined, with clear recognition of any relevant parameters. For misconstruing an entity by ascribing inappropriate qualities or considering it out of context engenders misconception. Though particulars may be enumerable only to an infinite intellect, one should strive to understand essential general principles. Since generalities intrinsically contain innumerable details, properly grasping a key universal concept enlightens one to the truth of myriads of particulars subsumed within it, suddenly recognizing each one that becomes known through its self-evident belonging to that broader reality. As our sages advise, "One should always have matters of Torah as generalities, not particulars."

Yet general principles must also be properly understood in their full scope and aspects. No detail is truly negligible or unworthy of concern, for nothing exists devoid of consequence at some level. While some specifics may be irrelevant in certain contexts, their impact elsewhere remains significant, given the all-encompassing nature of each general truth that must suffice in every respect. Careful attention and precise tracing of the progression through which each detail flows from prior elements and coalesces into subsequent effects is therefore imperative, that one may gain true wisdom and enlightenment.

Accordingly, dear reader, I have composed this work to elucidate the foundations of faith and service definitively, in a clear systematic manner facilitating authentic comprehension of these pivotal principles in all their aspects, saved from confusion. Herein their roots and branches are bared, interrelations explained, such that they take root and become absorbed within your heart and soul, for the perfection of your mind and being. From this basis, attainment of the knowledge of God throughout Torah, and comprehension of all its hidden treasures, will readily unfold through divine blessing.

I have diligently endeavored to present the ideas in a compelling progression, and language optimally expressive, to impart an accurate picture of these essential ideas I wish to share. Therefore, gentle friend, I ask that you likewise examine this work carefully, hold fast to its guidance, and do not overlook any detail, that no indispensable matter elude you. But delve thoroughly into its words to grasp each concept in its full depth of meaning, that its truths permeate your consciousness, and you find the tranquil clarity for which your soul surely yearns.

This text's title, Derech Hashem, meaning "God and His Ways or The Way of God," reflects its focus: the path of divine truth revealed by the prophets and in the Torah, through which He shapes reality and guides humankind. Correspondingly, this work unfolds in four sections: first, the foundations of existence; second, God's providence; third, prophecy; and fourth, proper service. May each word awaken within you vision and understanding, that you may walk amidst the wonders of His wisdom and ways.

Therefore my brother, who genuinely seek closeness with Hashem, take this as your guide, that God be with you. For He bestows discerning eyes and attentive ears to glimpse the hidden marvels embedded in Torah's every layer of meaning.

Part 1 - The Creator

Summary of Part 1

Part 1 - Chapter 1

God's existence is singular, necessary, independent, and intrinsically perfect beyond grasp. His essence precludes deficiencies and is the true cause of all existents. His perfection is only known through tradition and investigation. As the root of existence, deficiencies are inherently absent from Him. His unique existence is the cause of all other existents. Created things cannot be inferred about Him since their natures are not equivalent. Six foundational cognitions about God's existence have been established: its truth, perfection, necessity, independence, simplicity and unity.

Part 1 - Chapter 2

The purpose of creation is bestowing goodness. For completeness, recipients must earn goodness through free will, made possible by being balanced between perfection and deficiency. Had Adam not sinned, he would have perfected himself and the world, meriting eternal delight. Man establishes his level of perfection and proximity to God through choices. The dynamics of perfection and deficiency exist so man can obtain one and remove the other through his efforts.

Part 1 - Chapter 3

Man was given a divine soul and earthly body with free choice between good and evil. Adam's sin added deficiencies requiring death and resurrection for ultimate perfection. The soul strengthens through good deeds, preparing to purify the rebuilt body and cling to God. Two states of man are examined: before and after Adam's sin, which greatly reduced him. Death and resurrection were decreed. The soul benefits from the separation, readying to finally purify the body.

Part 1 - Chapter 4

Though immersed in matter, man can attain perfection through Torah and mitzvot which perfect man and rectify creation. Divine service aims to strengthen the soul and perfect the body through proper worldly endeavors. Torah study as the foremost means enables man to draw divine influence based on comprehension. Proper orientation of worldly endeavors elevates man from within matter itself.

Part 1 - Chapter 5

Creation comprises interconnected spiritual and physical realms. Two fundamental movements permeate creation: natural top-down and volitional bottom-up. Evil exists for man to overcome through free will, stemming from divine concealment. Its revelation eliminates evil and perfects creation. This world prepares for the next through good deeds. Divine illumination versus concealment underlie good and evil forces.

Chapter 1 - The Existence of God

Every Jew must believe and know that there exists a first Being, eternal and everlasting, who brought into existence and continues to bring into existence all that exists, and He is God, blessed be He.

It must also be known that the truth of this Being, blessed be He, is completely beyond grasp by anything other than Him. Only this is known about Him: that He is a perfect Being in all manners of perfection, and absolutely no deficiency exists in Him. These matters we know through tradition from the Patriarchs and Prophets. All of Israel attained them at the event of Mount Sinai and stood firmly upon their truth. They taught them to their children throughout the generations, as Moses our teacher commanded by the mouth of the Almighty—"Lest you forget the things your eyes beheld etc. You shall make them known to your children and grandchildren."[1]

However, all these matters are also proven true by intellectual investigation through conclusive proofs. It will be shown to be necessary that they are so, from the existent beings and their conceptions that we see with our eyes, according to the science of nature, geometry, astronomy, and other sciences. From them will be taken true premises which will yield a demonstration of these true matters. However, we will not elaborate on this now, but only present the premises for their truth. Then, we will arrange the matters clearly, according to the tradition in our possession and what is well known throughout our nation.

It must be known that the existence of this Being, blessed be He, is a necessary existence, that it is completely impossible for Him not to exist.

It must also be known that His existence does not depend on anything else whatsoever; rather, His existence is necessary of itself.

Similarly, it must be known that the existence of God is a simple, unique existence without any composition or multiplicity. All perfection exists within Him in a simple manner. Meaning that as it is for the soul, where are found many varied powers, each of which has its own definition. For example, memory is one power, desire is another power, as is imagination, and none of these enters into the definition of the other at all. The faculty of memory is one definition, and desire is another, and desire does not enter into the definition of memory, nor memory into the definition of desire, and so on for all of them.

However, God, blessed be He, does not possess varied powers, even though in truth there are within Him varied matters—for He indeed desires. He is wise, powerful, and perfect with all perfection. However, the truth of His existence is a singular matter that truly includes within its truth and definition— meaning the truth of its matter—that all perfection is necessarily inherent within it and all deficiencies are necessarily absent from it.

It turns out that all perfection exists within Him not as something added onto His essence and the truth of His matter, but rather due to the truth of His matter itself, which includes all perfection within its truth, for it is impossible for that matter to exist without all perfection inherently.

Behold, in truth, this approach is extremely beyond our grasp and conception. We have virtually no way to explain it nor words to expound it. Our conception and imagination encompass only compound matters bounded by the nature created from Him, for that is what our senses sense and bring the conception of to the intellect.

But in creations, the matters are many and separate. However, we have already prefaced that the truth of His existence is beyond grasp. Nothing can be inferred about the Creator from what is observed in creations, for their matters and existence are not at all equivalent such that we could deduce from one about the other. But this too is from the matters known through tradition, as stated, and proven true through investigation of nature itself, in its laws and dynamics.

For it is certainly impossible that a singular Being found, devoid of all nature's laws, boundaries, and limitations; devoid of any absence or deficiency; of any multiplicity or composition; of any relativity or finite measure; and of any of the attributes of creations. He would be the true cause for all existents and all generated within them. For without this, the existence of these beings we observe and their continuity would have been impossible.

It also must be known that this Being, blessed be He, must necessarily be one and no more. Meaning, it is impossible for multiple existents whose existence is necessary of themselves to exist, but only a singular one must exist with this kind of necessary perfect existence. If any other existents are found, they will only exist because He wills them into existence through His will. All existents would depend on Him and not exist of themselves.

It turns out that these foundational cognitions are six, and they are: the truth of His existence, His perfection, the necessity of His existence, His independence, His simplicity, and His unity.

Chapter 2 - The Purpose of Creation

The purpose of creation is the bestowal of goodness from His own abundance, blessed be He, unto something other than Himself. When you consider this, you realize that He alone, blessed be He, embodies true perfection, completely free from any deficiency. There is no other form of perfection that can compare to His.

Consequently, any form of perfection separate from His is not genuine perfection. It is only termed as perfection in comparison to something that has more flaws. However, absolute perfection is nothing but His own, blessed be He. Thus, His desire to bestow goodness upon another cannot be fulfilled by giving just some goodness; He must give the ultimate good that a creation can receive.

Since He alone is the embodiment of true good, His desire to do good can only be fulfilled by allowing another to partake in that very same inherent good, which is the complete and true good. However, this good is found only in Him. His wisdom, therefore, decreed that the realization of this bestowal should be through providing a space for creations to connect with Him, to the extent of their ability.

This means that although it is impossible for them to attain the same level of perfection as His, by connecting with Him, they can achieve a certain degree of that perfection. They can delight in that true goodness, to the extent that they are capable. Thus, the intention of God in creation is for it to delight in His goodness, to the extent possible.

Nevertheless, His wisdom has determined that for the good to be complete, the recipient of this delight must possess the good themselves. In other words, they must acquire this good on their own, not simply receive it by chance. This resembles, to a certain extent, His own perfection. For He, blessed be He, is inherently perfect, not by chance. Perfection is an intrinsic part of Him, and deficiencies are inherently absent from Him, because of the true nature of His being.

God's wisdom has decreed that for the good to be complete, the one delighting in it must take possession of that good themselves. This means that they must acquire the good through their own efforts, not just stumble upon it. This is a semblance of God's own inherent perfection, not a perfection that just happens to be there. For God is perfect by His very nature, without any deficiencies. His very essence demands perfection and excludes any flaws. However, nothing besides God can possess this inherent nature. To somewhat resemble Him, a being must at least strive for perfection on their own, not have it imposed upon them, and eliminate any potential deficiencies.

Therefore, God has arranged for both perfection and deficiency to be possible outcomes. He created beings with the potential for both, providing them with the means to attain perfection and eradicate deficiencies on their own. In doing so, they resemble their Creator as closely as possible, making them worthy of connecting with Him and delighting in His goodness.

Furthermore, as these created beings strive for perfection and increasingly resemble their Creator, they also draw closer to Him. This process continues until achieving perfection and being in close connection with Him become one and the same. This is because His existence, blessed be He, is the epitome of true perfection. Therefore, any form of inherent perfection belongs solely to Him, like a branch originates from a root. Although the branch may not reach the original perfection of the root, it is nonetheless an extension and result of that initial perfection.

You can see that true perfection belongs only to His existence, and any deficiency is simply the concealment of His goodness and the hiding of His presence. The revelation of His presence and closeness to Him are the root causes of all perfection. Conversely, the hiding of His presence is the root cause of all deficiencies. The degree of His presence determines the level of perfection, and its absence results in deficiency.

Humanity stands balanced, influenced by the revelation or concealment of God's presence. By actively pursuing perfection and acquiring it through their own efforts, humans grab hold of Him, who is the source of all perfection. The more they perfect themselves, the stronger their connection and closeness to Him become. Eventually, the ultimate achievement of perfection and the ultimate closeness to Him become synonymous, resulting in delight in His goodness and true perfection.

For these dynamics of perfection and deficiency to exist, and for humanity to have the capacity for both as well as the ability to acquire one and remove the other – and for the means towards this perfection to be accessible – there must be a myriad of details in creation. These details are interrelated until the ultimate purpose is fully realized. However, the creation intended for this grand purpose of connection with God is deemed the primary creation. Everything else in existence serves to assist this primary creation in achieving its ultimate purpose.

Specifically, humans represent the true primary creation. All other creations, whether of a higher or lower order, exist solely to aid humanity in fulfilling its complete spiritual purpose in all its varied aspects and requirements. We will delve deeper into this topic later, God willing. For now, understand that wisdom and virtuous character traits are aspects of perfection, meant to refine humanity. Physicality and imagination, on the other hand, are aspects of deficiency, between which humans navigate to achieve their own state of perfection.

Chapter 3 - The Human Species

We have already mentioned that man is that creation created to cling to Him, and he is placed between perfection and deficiency, with ability to acquire perfection. However, this must be through his own choice and will. For if he were compelled in his actions to certainly choose perfection, at minimum, he would not truly be called master of his perfection, since he does not own it, as he was compelled by another to acquire it - and the one compelling it would be its master, not him. The supernal intent would not be fulfilled. Therefore, it was necessary that the matter be left to his choice, that his inclination be balanced equally towards both sides, not compelled towards either of them. That he possesses the power of choice, to choose deliberately whichever of them he wants, with the ability in his hands to acquire whichever of them he wants. Therefore, man was created with an evil inclination and good inclination, and the choice is in his hands to incline himself to whichever side he wants.

However, for this matter to be completed properly, the supernal wisdom decreed that man be composed of two opposites - an intellectual, pure soul, and an earthy, turbid body. Each of them would naturally incline to its side - the body to physicality and the soul to intellect. A battle would be found between them, such that if the soul overcomes, it and the body with it become elevated. That person attains the intended perfection. But if man allows the physical to overcome him, the body becomes lowly, and his soul with it. That person is unfit for perfection, and becomes distanced from it, heaven forfend. This man has the ability to subjugate his physicality before his intellect and soul, and acquire his perfection, as stated.

His goodness decreed that there be a limit to this endeavor required of man to attain perfection. Upon completing his endeavor he would attain his perfection and rest in his eternal delight. Therefore two time periods were designated - one, a time of work, and two, a time of receiving reward. The attribute of goodness is abundant, for the work has a legislated time, according to what His wisdom decreed fitting for it. However, receiving reward has no end; he increasingly delights for eternity in the perfection he acquired.

According to the changing times, his state and other incidents must change. For during the entire time of endeavor, he must be in a particular state that contains all the necessary conditions for this endeavor. This means that the battle between intellect and matter is necessary. Nothing prevents matter from ruling to its fitting degree, nor does anything prevent intellect from ruling appropriately. There is also nothing that causes matter or intellect to strengthen more than is appropriate. Although one way might seem better, it is not ideal according to the true intent for man, which is to achieve perfection through his own efforts. During the time of receiving reward, it is fitting for him to have a state opposite to this. At that time, if matter ruled, it would only have darkened and impeded the soul from clinging to God. Therefore, it is fitting that then only the soul should rule, and matter should follow it completely, so it does not impede in any way. Thus, two worlds were created - this world and the next. This world's place and natural system suit man for the entire time of endeavor. The next world's place and system suit him during the time of receiving reward.

What still needs to be known is that the human species' primary purpose is not as we see it now, for a great change occurred with Adam Harishon's sin, which altered man and the world from their initial state. The details of this change and its consequences are many, and we will discuss them later, God willing. Thus, the discussion of the human species and its topics is twofold: before the sin, and after the sin, as we will explain further, God willing.

Adam Harishon at the time of his creation was in the state we have mentioned so far. He was composed of two opposite parts: the soul and the body. In existence were the matters of good and evil, and he stood balanced between them to cleave to whichever he wished. It was fitting for him to choose good, strengthen his soul over his body, and his intellect over his matter. Then he would have been perfected immediately and rested in his completeness eternally.

You need to know that although we do not sense any action of the soul in the body except for life and intellect, in truth, the soul can purify the body and elevate it until it becomes worthy to delight in completeness. Adam Harishon would have achieved this had he not sinned. His soul would have purified his body until it was purified enough to be established in eternal delight.

When he sinned, things changed significantly. Initially, there were deficiencies in Creation necessary for Adam Harishon to be in the balanced state we mentioned and have room to earn completeness through labor. However, his sin added and multiplied deficiencies in man himself and the entire Creation, making rectification more difficult. Initially, it was easy for him to emerge from his inherent deficiency and acquire completeness, as things were arranged according to the attribute of goodness and fairness.

Since man was not the cause of the evil and deficiency within him but was created with it inherently, when he would distance himself from evil and turn to good, he would immediately emerge from the deficiency and acquire completeness. However, through his sin, since completeness was further concealed, deficiencies multiplied, and he was the cause of his own evil, it would no longer be easy for him to return, emerge from deficiency, and acquire completeness. The necessary effort on his part now to reach completeness is doubled; first, he and the world need to return to the state they were in before the sin, and afterward, elevate from that state to the state of completeness that man was destined to ascend to.

Furthermore, God's attribute of justice decreed that neither man nor the world would be able to reach completeness while still in their damaged form. They would necessarily need to undergo destruction, meaning death for man and destruction for all other corrupted beings. The soul can only purify the body after departing from it when the body dies and decomposes. Then it will be rebuilt in a new structure, the soul will enter it, and purify it. Similarly, the entire world will be destroyed from its current form and be rebuilt in another form fit for completeness. Therefore, man was sentenced to die and come back to life, which is the matter of the resurrection of the dead. The world was sentenced to be destroyed and then renewed, which is what the sages said, that the world exists for six thousand years and is destroyed, and at the end of the thousand years, God renews His world[1].

According to this principle, the time of true reward, the time of receiving the reward we mentioned earlier, and its place is after the resurrection in the renewed world. There, man will delight with his body and soul, his body purified by his soul and prepared by it to delight in that goodness. People will be differentiated there, their status and level will change according to the extent they toiled in the world of deeds and according to how much they strove to attain completeness. For according to this measure, the soul itself will shine and illuminate the body and purify it. Both will acquire preciousness and elevation and be worthy of drawing near the Master, blessed be He, shining with the light of His countenance and delighting in His true goodness.

---

[1] Sanhedrin 97a

Since death was decreed upon man, this composite being must separate for a time, then reunite. It is, therefore, fitting that there be a place for both separating parts, suitable for the purpose of that separation. The body must return to its elements; its composition must decompose and its form be destroyed. It came from dust, and to dust, it shall return, as God said to man[2].

However, the soul that merits through its deeds waits until the body's necessary tasks are completed. This includes decomposition and destruction at first, remaining in the earth for the required duration, and then rebuilding when it can reenter the body. It needs an interim place, for which the world of souls was prepared. Meritorious souls enter this realm after leaving the body, residing there in a restful place until the body's necessary processes conclude. During this time, those souls reside in elevation and delight, resembling the true reward mentioned earlier. Their level in the world of souls aligns with their earthly deeds, which also determine their later reward. Yet, true perfection for those who merit it will not be attained by either body or soul alone, but through their reunion after resurrection.

Besides being a waiting place for souls during the body's absence, the world of souls offers great benefits to the souls and, subsequently, the body. After the decree that man reaches completeness only after death, despite his deeds in life hinting that without death he would not attain world's perfection—for

____

[2] Bereshit. 3,19

the time of acquiring completeness is only in this world before death—it follows that the soul, while in the body, where evil clings inseparably, remains dark and dim. Through good deeds, the soul acquires precious perfection, but it cannot shine as it deserves; everything remains suppressed until it can emerge. The impediment lies not with the soul but with the body; the body loses out because it does not receive the purification it should. The soul, too, loses, for it is suppressed and cannot shed its radiance or purify the body as it should. Yet, this action would bring the soul great perfection, as perfection lies in improving another. A creation achieves perfection by performing its intended role, and it lacks perfection until it does so.

When the soul departs for the world of souls, it shines according to its deeds. There it strengthens what was weakened in the body, preparing for what it will do upon resurrection. When it returns to the body at the proper time, it can perform its fitting action—purification. However, when the soul enters a fetus's body, even without having achieved perfection, its innate preciousness and radiance would be enough to greatly purify the matter, exceeding the human realm.

But divine decree suppresses and conceals its power, so this does not happen. Instead, it resides in the body, shrouded, acting in the measure desired by divine wisdom. As it performs good deeds, it should spread and shine, purifying the body. Yet, according to the earlier decree, this can only happen in the world of souls.

Upon returning to the body after resurrection, the soul will not be diminished or concealed but will enter with full radiance and power. It will purify the body immensely and immediately, without the gradual development children require. However, this will not preclude further elevations for the body and soul together, fitting for their level.

The soul's immediate entry into the body post-resurrection will make the person precious and exalted, his body receiving an initial purification and elevation beyond anything in his previous lifetime. This purification, based on his good deeds, places him at the level he deserves among those who merit completeness. The body and soul will then ascend further, fitting for their level.

Chapter 4 - Man's State in This World

In man's state in this world, two matters will be examined: the constitution of man himself in his parts and composition, and the place he is set in with everything accompanying it. Regarding man himself, we have already mentioned how he is a composite of two opposites that were compounded within him, which are the soul and the body. We see clearly that his materiality and its offshoots are very strong within him, for immediately after his birth, he is almost entirely material, with intellect acting only minimally. As he grows, intellect progresses and strengthens in each person according to his matters, but in any case, materiality does not cease ruling him and bending him to its matters. Rather, if he grows in wisdom and studies it and strengthens himself in its paths, he will make an effort to conquer his nature, not loosen the reins of his desires from his hand, and strengthen himself to follow the paths of intellect. However, the inner dynamics of these matters that we see are as follows: In the existence of matter and its essence, turbidity and darkness are found inherently; it is an existence extremely distant and opposite of what truly draws near God, may He be blessed, and attaches to His holiness.

The soul itself, even though it is pure and supernal in itself, when it enters the material, turbid body and becomes enmeshed in it, it finds itself estranged and repelled from its natural purpose to an opposite purpose, constrained in it with overpowering force, unable to emerge from it except by exerting a force stronger than the force constraining it. Since the Master, blessed be He, decreed that this combination of man's body and soul will never separate - for the separation of death is only temporary until the resurrection of the dead, but afterward, the soul must return to the body, and the two will exist eternally together - the soul is compelled to make an effort and strengthen itself, progressively weakening the power of the material darkness, until the body remains unobscured. Then it [the soul] will be able to rise with it [the body] and shine with the supernal light, as opposed to how it [the soul] was darkened and debased along with it [the body] initially. Man's state in this world is one where the material is strong within him as stated, with the material being turbid and dark, man finds himself in great darkness, extremely distant from what he should be - attached and clinging to God. Indeed, with this, he must direct his effort to strengthen his soul against the power of his matter, improve his state, elevating himself elevation after elevation to the appropriate level.

The place in which he is situated is also material and dark, and all the beings within it are material, and man's occupation with it and its contents cannot be anything but material and corporeal since they are all material and corporeal. Man's own constitution and the composition of his parts compel this occupation for him, for he cannot exist without eating and drinking and all the other natural matters, nor without money and property in order to attain these needs. Thus, it turns out that whether due to man's body, or his world, or his occupation, he is embedded in matter and sunk into its darkness, and he will need great effort and strong diligence to elevate himself from this state to a pure and lofty one, yet he is compelled by his nature regarding these material matters.

However, from the depth of His supernal wisdom, God arranged for things to be in a way that even though man is by necessity sunk in matter as we have written, he can still attain perfection and elevation to purity and heights from within matter itself and corporeal occupation. On the contrary, his lowliness will be his exaltation, and from there he will acquire preciousness and honor unlike any other, by transforming darkness into light and gloom into radiance. This is because God set boundaries and systems for man regarding his use of the world and its creations, and the intent he should have with them. When man makes use of them within those boundaries and systems and with that intent that the Creator commanded, that very corporeal and material action itself becomes an action of perfection, and through it existence of perfection and great sublimity intensifies within man, and he is elevated from his lowly state and raised up from it.

The supernal wisdom observed all the general deficiencies within human nature, and all the matters of true value and greatness necessary for humans to be worthy of uniting with God and reveling in His goodness. To address this, He established systems and set boundaries for humans. By adhering to these, the necessary elements of true greatness we mentioned will be intensified within them, and all that hinders unity with the Divine will be eliminated from their lives. Had death not been decreed upon humans, as we have previously noted, these actions would have fortified the soul and diminished the body's darkness, eventually purifying the body completely. Together, the soul and body would have ascended to unite with God. But since the decree of death was issued, this purification does not happen all at once. However, the soul does strengthen, and the body becomes potentially purified, with actual perfection emerging in due time.

These systems and boundaries are essentially the positive and negative commandments. Each commandment aims to instill and enhance a level of true greatness within humans, and to remove elements of darkness and deficiency, either by performing a positive commandment or abstaining from a negative one. The details of all the commandments, as well as each individual commandment, are based on the truth of human existence and the necessary elements of perfection, each within its own conditions and requirements for completion. The supernal wisdom, fully aware of all truths, observed everything and included all that was needed in the commandments given to us in His Torah.

The essence of divine service is that humans constantly turn to their Creator, recognizing that they were created solely to unite with Him, and are placed in this world to overcome their instincts and subject themselves to their Creator through intellect, contrary to material desires and tendencies. They should direct all their actions towards this ultimate goal without deviation. This conduct is two-fold: first, what they do because God commanded it, and second, what they do out of necessity for their needs. The first is about obedience to God's commands, and the second is about responsibly using the world to meet their needs. The use of the world should align with God's will, focusing on the health of the body and sustaining life optimally, not on indulging material desires. The aim is to prepare the body as a vessel for the soul's service to its Creator, without any hindrance from its unpreparedness or weakness.

When humans use the world in this manner, this very act becomes one of perfection, garnering true value just as through the fulfillment of commandments. For this is also commanded of us: to care for our bodies properly so that we can serve our Creator with them. Thus, we elevate not only ourselves but also the world by using it to aid in our service to the Creator.

The love and reverence for the Creator are what humans must strengthen within themselves, by reflecting on God's magnificence and human insignificance. This humility and longing to serve God lead to a purification of the material aspects and an enhancement of the soul's brightness, elevating humans step by step until they achieve closeness to Him.

Regarding Torah study, God has provided it as the highest means of drawing humans closer to Himself. It involves two aspects: contemplation and understanding. In His kindness, God gave us a structured composition of words, which make up the Torah and the books of the Prophets. Those who contemplate these words with purity and focused intent, aiming to fulfill

God's will, will greatly enhance supreme greatness and perfection within themselves. Those who strive to comprehend the meanings and explanations will gain perfection progressively according to their efforts.

Even more so, those who penetrate the hidden depths and secrets of these texts will embed within their souls a profound level of greatness and perfection. Through these engagements, not only do humans gain greatness and perfection for themselves, but they also elevate and perfect the existence of all creation, specifically through the Torah.

The inner purpose of all commandments is to draw closer to God and to shine with His light, while avoiding transgressions is to prevent distancing from Him. This is their true intent. However, there are many detailed laws concerning these, related to the complexities of human and creation's nature, as mentioned. We shall explore some of these in detail later, with God's assistance.

Chapter 5 - Physical and Spiritual

The components of all creation are divided into two: physical and spiritual. The physical are those perceptible to our senses, and are subdivided into higher and lower. The higher are the entirety of the heavenly bodies, meaning the spheres and their stars. The lower are the entirety of what is in the hollow of the lower sphere, meaning the earth, the waters, the air, and everything contained within them of perceptible bodies.

The spiritual are created beings devoid of physicality, imperceptible to our senses, and are divided into two types: Souls and Separates. Souls are a type of spiritual created being destined to enter a body, to be constrained within it and to bind to it in a strong connection, and to perform various actions within it at different times.

Separates are a type of spiritual created being not destined for bodies at all, and are divided into two sections: the first called Forces, the second Angels. They too have many and various levels, and have natural laws of existence according to their levels and ranks, such that we can actually call them many species of the first type, which is the angelic type.

However, there is found one species of created being which is like an intermediary between spiritual and physical, meaning that it is truly imperceptible to our senses, and also is not constrained by any of the constraints of perceptible physicality and its laws, and in this regard it is inaccurately called spiritual. But it differs in its matter from the angelic type, even though it resembles it in some aspects, and it has particular laws and distinct boundaries according to its true existence. This species is called demonic, the species of demons. However, it too subdivides into other details, with the general species being a type relative to them, as they are species under it.

The human species alone is distinguished and separated out, to be composed of two completely different kinds of creation, which are the supernal soul and the lowly body, something not found in any other creature. Here you must be careful not to err and think the matter of other living creatures is like that of man, for the soul of living creatures is nothing but a fine material thing, which is also found in man, in the aspect of his being a living creature. However, beyond all this man has a supernal soul, which is its own kind of creation, completely separate from the body, extremely distant from it, which comes and binds itself to it by divine decree, for the purpose we mentioned in previous sections.

The physical created beings are known to us, and their general natural laws and ordinances are well-known. However, we cannot properly conceive the spiritual beings, for they are beyond our imagination, and we will only discuss them and their matters according to the tradition we possess. Now, one of the great fundamental principles we possess in this matter is that corresponding to everything found in the lowly created beings, there exist higher, separate forces, from which the lowly emanate and emerge in a certain singular order of emanation that the wisdom of God decreed, these lowly ones and their incidents. And these forces are the roots to these lowly created beings, and the lowly created beings are branches and offshoots of those forces, and are interconnected like the links of a chain.

We also have a tradition that trustees were appointed over each and every object and incident within these lowly created beings, from the angelic type we mentioned above, whose role is to sustain that object or incident in the lowly existence as it is, and to renew what is fitting to be renewed in the lowly according to the supernal decree.

The primary existence of the world and its true state is in those supernal forces, and what occurs in the lowly physicals is a consequence of what is in them. This applies both to what occurred at the start of creation, and what renews with the changing of times. Meaning, according to what was created of those forces and the system they were arranged in and the boundaries they were given, so was what consequently emanated, according to the law of emanation that the Creator desired. According to what renews and is renewed within them, so is what renews and is renewed in the lowly realm. However, existence, state, order, and all other distinctions in the forces, are according to what pertains to them based on their true matter. Existence, state, order, and all other incidents in the lowly realm, emanate and translate into what pertains to them based on their true matter.

Therefore, the principle suggests that all existences originate from the supernal forces and culminate below. All things that are renewed start above and end below. An exception to this rule concerns human free will. The universe's Master granted humans the freedom to choose between good and evil. In doing so, He endowed them with the power to influence the world and its beings based on their choices.

Thus two opposite general movements are found in the world - the first is natural compelled, the second is volitional. The first is from above downwards, the second from below upwards. The compelled is the movement by which the lowly are motivated by the supernal forces, and this is from above downwards. The volitional is what man motivates through his choice. Now, what he motivates cannot be anything but physical, for man is physical and his actions physical. But due to the connection and unification found between the supernal forces and the physical, when the physical is motivated, it will by consequence reach the supernal force above it, and this movement is found to be from below upwards, opposite the natural compelled mentioned.

The world knows two fundamental movements: the naturally compelled and the voluntary. The first movement is top-down, driven by supernal forces. The second, bottom-up, is driven by human choice. Man, being physical, can only affect physical entities. The link between the physical and the supernal means that when the former moves, the latter is impacted, creating a bottom-up movement opposite to the natural top-down one.

Yet, not all human actions are voluntary; some are influenced by supernal decrees for reward or punishment. Actions compelled by such decrees align with the top-down movement of the world, while voluntary actions initiate a bottom-up movement.

God has ordained that all matters subject to human choice will activate those forces to the level and rank they are destined. This activation comes not only from actions but also from speech and thought, limited by the boundaries set by divine wisdom. Following a voluntary act, a compelled movement must ensue; once the supernal forces are activated by humans, they, in turn, influence the lower entities. These interactions are governed by complex laws set by divine wisdom, which dictate the flow from humans to supernal forces and vice versa, influencing God's governance across all existence.

As divine wisdom has decreed the existence of both good and evil, the inception of this duality lies in the original forces, with the physical realm reflecting this state. The forces were arranged to exhibit deficiency and perfection, correlating with a state of being with or without divine illumination. Perfection in the supernal forces leads to goodness in the physical derivatives, and deficiency leads to the opposite.

It is vital to understand that the illumination of the divine presence is the true cause of all goodness, both in the supernal forces and their derivatives. Conversely, the absence of this illumination is the root cause of all evil. While the Creator is directly associated with all that is good, He is not directly linked to evil. Instead, the absence of divine light is seen as the root cause of evil. For the specifics of evil, the Creator, whose power is unlimited, has created a distinct root and source for the manifestation of evil as deemed necessary by divine wisdom for the desired state of humanity and the world.

This is what Scripture states: "Forming light and creating darkness, making peace and creating evil."[3] The core of this statement encompasses a variety of forces, which give rise to all forms of deficiencies and evils, affecting both the soul and the body, with all their complexities and varieties.

These universal forces are controlled by the degree to which His light is concealed and His presence hidden. The extent of this concealment dictates the level of permission and dominion granted to these forces, either collectively or in part, to exert their influence.

When these forces dominate, goodness is diminished, and the fundamental elements of creation we have discussed become corrupted, along with their offshoots. Conversely, when these forces are restrained and their influence revoked, goodness triumphs, and the foundations of creation are restored to a positive state, along with their offshoots.

The dynamics of good and evil, the conflict between intellect and matter, and the processes of restoration and corruption are

---

[3] Is.45,7

all rooted in the dominance or suppression of these forces and their impact on creation, from its origins to its extensions.

The evil forces mentioned have various levels and gradations, and what stems from them is generally termed impurity, darkness, and filth. In contrast, what results from the illumination of His countenance is known as holiness, purity, light, and blessing. To understand the nuances of these elements, we categorize and detail these general classes, which are all part of the divine governance with which the Almighty governs His world.

Angelic beings, as previously explained, are designated to manifest these forces into reality, whether for good or for ill. They are His servants, executing His will, for it is His desire that His decrees are carried out through these angels, in accordance with His plans and their assigned roles.

Part 2 - Providence

Summary of Part 2

Part 2 - Chapter 1

God's providence sustains all creations, each receiving according to its nature and purpose. Providence over humanity involves judgment for deeds due to free will. God watches over and judges matters then issues consequences accordingly through systems He ordained. Providence over humanity differs since they are actors, not just passive recipients.

Part 2 - Chapter 2

This world prepares for the next. Sins necessitate punishment but judgment aims for ultimate perfection. Things occur according to precise justice. Suffering refines; the wicked exhaust merits here. The future gathering has levels based on deeds. Judgment is divided between this world, the soul world, and after resurrection. Only God knows precise laws. We know the general systems and their basis.

Part 2 - Chapter 3

Fortunes test and ease service. Sufferings awaken sinners and refine the righteous who suffer for others. Reasons include: testing, reward, awakening, collective benefit. All is judged precisely as things truly are. Providence oversees all factors. Outcomes consider one's state and contemporaries. Suffering atones for one's generation. The righteous mend corruption.

Part 2 - Chapter 4

Israel was chosen while nations remain lowly. Their merits aid them, but the wicked exhaust theirs. Their judgment is less direct, overseen by angels. Noahide laws were given. Israel's redemption revealed their superiority. The wicked perish; the righteous delight eternally. Nations influence themselves, not God's governance. Individuals are judged by deeds. Providence can override for Israel's needs.

Part 2 - Chapter 5

God's providence follows precise order, occasionally overriding nature through miracles. All is sustained directly by Him. Conduits interact with the physical world according to their natures and roles. Miracles override nature as He wills. At creation, God revealed the unfolding of miracles to the spiritual roots.

Part 2 - Chapter 6

Matters are judged in heavenly courts. God appoints angels to oversee events. Accusations prompt judgments. Judgment follows precise order. God heads courts, angels argue merits, God finalizes verdicts. Satan accuses within designated parameters. Judgments have detailed laws of times and procedures.

Part 2 - Chapter 7

Stars influence mundane matters but can be overridden. Their predictions have limits. Stars enable manifestation from spiritual roots to physical branches. They dictate mundane outcomes but can be overridden per God's will. Their partial laws provide limited foresight. Israel is not fully under their influence.

Part 2 - Chapter 8

Justice originates in love. Sometimes mercy overrides law. Emanation influences body and soul. Four spiritual states reflect progress of humanity. Reward and punishment express justice and divine uniqueness. Divine emanation physically and spiritually influences the world's states. Four levels mark human progression: ignorance, intellect without prophecy, intellect with prophecy, universal prophecy.

Chapter 1 - Regarding God's Providence in General

It is known and explained that all creatures, both supernal and lower, were created because the Supreme Wisdom saw need and benefit in them for the overall purpose of creation. All their natural laws and properties were decreed and instilled as the Supreme Wisdom determined fitting, according to the intent it aimed for in that particular creature. For that same reason they were created, it is also fitting that they exist for as long as they are beneficial for the entirety of creation. Therefore, the Lord, blessed be He, who created all these creatures, will also not refrain from watching over them to sustain them in the state He wants them in.

We have already mentioned in Part 1, Chapter 5, that the beginning of all creatures are the separate forces, and from them the physical bodies emanate. The matters in the physical bodies in all their details derive from what was imparted to them from those forces in their specific aspects, and there is no small or large thing in the physical that does not have a cause and root in the separate forces according to their aspects. The Lord, blessed be He, watches over all these matters as He created them, meaning firstly over the separate forces, and over their entire chain of causation as it truly is. Similarly, He also watches over the angels He appointed over the creations, to sustain them and their mission and to perpetuate the power through which they act.

However, since the human species is different from all other species, in that it was given free choice and ability regarding what pertains to its perfection or deficiency. It is found in this aspect to be actor and mover and not one acted upon.

Providence over it must also differ from providence over other species, which are passive and not active, and are only as appropriate for the completion of that species as rooted in its source. The Creator oversees and observe the details of their deeds, to act consequently according to their ways and actions. Thus all their deeds and their consequences will be overseen, and will in turn be watched over according to what is fitting as consequences of those deeds in detail, measure for measure.

This is not applicable to other species, whose members are passive and not active, and are only as their source and its offshoots dictate they should naturally be. Providence over them is to sustain that source and its branches as the nature and law of the source dictates they will be. But the human species, whose members are actors and movers, requires particular oversight according to what their actions cause for them, no less and no more.

Chapter 2 - Man in This World

We have already mentioned that the purpose of creating the human species is that it should merit and arrive at the true good, which is clinging to God in the next world. Thus the end of all its cycles is the repose of the next world. However, the Supreme Wisdom decreed fitting and proper that preceding this should be its state in this world, bound and limited by the laws of nature of this world, for this is the true and fitting preparation for attaining the desired purpose.

According to this principle, all matters of this world were arranged to be a preparation and invitation for what will later be in the perfected world, which is the world to come.

This preparation revolves around two poles: the individual and the general. The individual is the matter of each person acquiring their perfection through their deeds, and the general is the whole human species preparing for the next world. The explanation of this matter is that since the human species was created with inclination, impulse, and choice, it is unavoidable that among its parts there will be good and evil. The end of this cycle must be that the evil will be rejected and the good gathered, making of them one whole, for which the next world with its true comprehended goodness will be prepared.

However, the rule of choice, which necessitates the possibility we mentioned of good and evil among parts of humankind, also necessitates the same possibility in the deeds of each individual person, that they could be all good or all evil, or some good and some evil. This is an impediment to gathering the perfect ones we mentioned, for already in one individual there are found good matters and evil matters. To oversee some of them and not the rest, even if those overseen are the majority, is not just. For the line of law dictates that all deeds should be rewarded, whether great or small, many or few.

Therefore, the Supreme Wisdom decreed dividing the reward, both for merit and punishment, into two times and two places. Meaning, all deeds will be divided into majority and minority, with only the majority judged in its fitting place and time, and the minority in its fitting place and time. The true and essential reward will be in the next world, as stated. The reward will be the worthy person remaining eternally clinging to God, and the punishment will be separation from the true good and destruction.

However, judgement regarding this will only be according to the majority of deeds. Good deeds of the wicked and bad deeds of the righteous, being the minority, will find reward and punishment in this world with its successes and troubles. The wicked will receive reward for the minority of their merits through their successes, and the righteous will receive punishment for their sins through suffering. Thus justice will be complete in all, leaving the matter regarding the next world as fitting for that perfect state - meaning only the righteous will remain without admixture of wicked, without impediments to the enjoyment prepared for them, and the wicked will be rejected and destroyed, with no claim left to them.

His infinite mercy also decreed increasing salvation for humankind, by making another kind of refinement possible for those fitting for it - meaning for those in whom evil has greatly overpowered, but not so much that their judgment is complete destruction. This includes the concept of Hell. Its purpose is to punish the sinner according to their sins, such that after the punishment, no debt remains regarding the evil deed done, and afterwards they can receive true reward according to their other good deeds. Through this the truly lost will be minimal, not massive, for they will only be those in whom evil has strengthened to such great extent that they have no place whatsoever to remain in true reward and eternal enjoyment.

Thus judgment is divided into three parts - its essence being the world after resurrection, but deeds deserving reward before then are of two types - those rewarded in this world and those in the world of souls. However, the details of this judgement are known only to the True Judge alone, for He alone knows the truth of deeds and their consequences in all their aspects and details, and knows what of them is fitting to reward at one time and in one way, and what at another time and way. What we know is only the general ways of this guidance, what it is based on and aims for.

As we have explained, the purpose of it all is to gather a complete collectivity that is worthy of eternal clinging to Him, and in order that this matter will be complete, all the preceding matters were necessary to prepare and arrange this purpose.

Looking deeper, you will see that besides resulting from justice as explained, this matter has another foundation - the created existence. This is because as we have explained, good deeds empower in a person, in body and soul, an existence of perfection and elevation; while bad deeds empower a turbid and deficient existence, each in precise accordance with the deeds, no less and no greater.

A righteous person, who has amassed a great measure of illumination and elevation, yet on the other hand has some intermixture of darkness and turbidity from a minority of bad deeds, this mixture as long as it remains in him, makes him unfit and unprepared for clinging to God. Therefore the supreme benevolence decreed a refinement for him, which is suffering, which God imbued with the possibility of removing that turbidity from the person, leaving them pure and clear, prepared for goodness at the fitting time.

According to the measure of turbidity a person accumulated through their deeds, so will be the suffering needed for their refinement. It is possible the suffering of the body will be insufficient to remove the turbidity from them, requiring spiritual suffering. All these general rules divide into many details, beyond human comprehension.

However, the completely wicked are those in whom the intense evil of their deeds has strengthened such great turbidity and darkness, that they are truly corrupted in body and soul, and have become unfit in any way to cling to Him. Even if they may have some good deeds, but in the scales of His righteousness these are not weighty enough to tip their side to true goodness at all - neither in quantity nor quality. For if these had tipped them to this, they would not be considered completely wicked, but rather those who get refined and progress until reaching a state ready for goodness. However, so that the attribute of justice should not be lacking, that these deeds remain without reward, it was decreed to give them their payment in this world, as mentioned, and that merit is exhausted and does not empower any true elevation in them.

Another crucial aspect of this matter is that the assembly of the righteous we mentioned for the future will not consist of individuals all at the same level of elevation and comprehension. The Supreme Wisdom has defined a lower limit, signifying the minimum level of attachment to Him and benefit from His perfection. Those whose deeds reach at least this minimal threshold will be included in that assembly, where they will eternally bask in His presence. However, those who fail to even attain this minimum will be completely separated and lost. Those who merit more will occupy higher positions within the assembly itself.

It is a fundamental part of His plan that each person should have complete mastery over their own goodness, both in a general and specific sense. This means that individuals will not attain goodness except through their own effort, and even the specific portion allocated to them will precisely correspond to their deeds. Consequently, a person will find themselves at no other level except the one they have chosen and placed themselves at. Within that assembly, there will undoubtedly be variations in height and importance, but a person's elevated or lowly status, greatness or smallness, will be solely determined by their own actions. Thus, there will be no cause for grievance against another.

Regarding the Law determining a person's position in the assembly of the next world, you will discover another significant distinction based on the evaluation of deeds and their consequences. Some deeds, according to the precise and just judgment, do not elevate a person in that assembly but are rewarded in this world. Consequently, these individuals remain at a lower level for eternity, on the periphery of that assembly.

This situation bears some resemblance to those we mentioned earlier, who receive their rewards in this world and are lost in the next. However, there are crucial differences. The completely wicked deplete the merits of their good deeds through worldly rewards and do not attain eternity at all. In contrast, these individuals secure an eternal existence through their deeds, even though they may require extensive spiritual refinement. Their portion in eternal existence, though, does not surpass the minimal share we mentioned.

Many of their merits are realized in this world. If these merits had been reserved for the next world instead of this one, they would have placed these individuals at a higher level in the assembly of the righteous.

However, everything we have discussed so far explains the suffering of the righteous in this world and the ease of the wicked, as well as spiritual punishments. This perspective focuses on preparing for the ultimate reward in the future. The goodness experienced by the righteous in this world follows a different path, which we will explain, God-willing.

Everything we have clarified aligns with the second, overarching aspect of preparation. Matters concerning the individual aspect follow a different course, which we will explore in a separate chapter, God-willing.

Chapter 3 – Individual Providence

As previously mentioned, the purpose assigned to each person is rooted in the coexistence of good and evil within the world. Humanity stands at the crossroads, with the freedom to choose the path of good. However, it's essential to understand that good and evil manifest in numerous forms. Every positive trait stems from the realm of good, while its counterpart finds its origins in evil. For instance, humility is a virtue, whereas pride is a vice. Compassion is a virtue, and cruelty is its evil counterpart. Contentment and happiness with one's circumstances are virtuous qualities, while their opposites represent aspects of evil. This distinction extends to all other traits and characteristics.

The Supreme wisdom meticulously considered all the nuances of these aspects that are compatible with human existence, as part of the overarching purpose mentioned earlier. It allowed them to manifest in various forms, encompassing their causes, contexts, and all associated elements, ingraining their potential within humanity.

For these aspects to exist and serve as tests, they required certain conditions among people. These conditions would provide the stage for both the manifestation of specific aspects of evil and the opportunity for individuals to resist them and understand their causes. For example, without disparities in wealth, there would be no chance for individuals to exhibit compassion or indifference. Rich individuals are tested by their wealth, determining whether they respond with indifference to the needy or extend compassion. Similarly, impoverished individuals face the test of contentment with their circumstances and gratitude towards their Creator, or the opposite.

Wealth serves as a test for the affluent, assessing whether they succumb to arrogance or worldly pursuits at the expense of serving their Creator. Alternatively, will they remain humble, prioritizing spiritual pursuits and moral values over materialism? These tests apply to various situations and traits.

The supreme wisdom has allocated these diverse tests to individuals as it deemed appropriate. Consequently, each person bears a unique role in their ongoing struggle against their own inclinations, which is their duty and responsibility in this world. They will be assessed based on their actions through divine judgment, accounting for the specific burdens they genuinely carry across all dimensions. This analogy is akin to servants of a king, all collectively working towards the betterment of the kingdom. Each servant has been assigned a specific role, and their individual responsibility lies in fulfilling their designated task. The king rewards them according to their performance in their respective roles. However, the intricacies and mechanisms of this division are beyond human comprehension, as only the supreme wisdom, transcending all intellectual capacity, has orchestrated them in the most perfect manner.

Considering that all aspects of the world transition from the abstract to the physical, as previously explained, the specifics of a person's tests and the associated elements originate in the abstract realm, shaped by their state of rectitude or corruption. Based on these abstract states, judgments are made, determining the corresponding physical manifestations tailored to each individual's unique suitability. Within this broader judgment, all entities align themselves at their designated levels.

The Supreme wisdom, in its omniscience, decreed what was fitting and just based on the genuine nature of things. This aligns with the fundamental principles we have previously discussed. The successes and challenges experienced in this world serve as tests. Consequently, the successes and adversities in this world serve as components of the trial individuals must undergo, based on the kinds of tests that supreme wisdom has deemed suitable for each person.

In addition to the individualized testing, there is another dimension involving divine justice and reward. The divine Judge has ordained that, as a consequence of one's deeds, they will receive divine assistance to facilitate their journey towards completeness and will be spared from certain obstacles. As stated in the verse, "He protects the steps of His pious ones."[4]

---

[4] Sam.2,9

Naturally, the level of assistance varies. One person, in accordance with their past deeds, may receive minimal divine aid, while another may benefit from far greater support, significantly easing their path to completeness. Conversely, there may be those who receive no divine assistance but also face no undue obstacles. Then, there are individuals who are subject to numerous obstacles due to their past actions, requiring substantial effort and dedication to overcome these hindrances and achieve completeness. Lastly, there are those who are entirely wicked, and every avenue of rectification seems blocked, leading them further down a path of rejection.

The nuances of these circumstances are multifaceted. For instance, a person may receive worldly success as a result of their merits, simplifying their divine service and removing obstacles on their path to completeness. Conversely, one's actions may lead to losses and hardships, creating additional hurdles that require considerable effort to surmount. For the wicked, they may experience unexpected successes that lead to their downfall, or conversely, suffer setbacks that prevent them from pursuing their wicked intentions. All of these situations align with divine wisdom, ensuring that everything is arranged in a manner that benefits all of creation. God judges all beings in accordance with their true nature, whether through ignorance or intent, whether complacency or willful disobedience. God's knowledge encompasses the authenticity of all actions, thoughts, and intentions, allowing for just judgment.

Another aspect to consider is suffering, which can serve various purposes. Sometimes, righteous individuals who have committed sins or those who have balanced their deeds may experience suffering to awaken them to repentance. This suffering serves as a wake-up call, urging them to return to a righteous path. It should be noted that this form of suffering differs from that which atones for sins, as it aims to prompt repentance rather than cleanse sins in this world. Punishments primarily exist due to the absence of repentance. Ideally, individuals should avoid sinning altogether, but if they do transgress, they should turn to repentance. Failure to heed this call may result in suffering intended to prevent their moral destruction. Initially, awakening suffering is experienced, and if it goes unheeded, the individual may then undergo purification suffering. As Elyahu said: "He opens their ears to discipline, exhorting them to turn away from sin."[5]

There is a limit to how long a sinner's continued sinful choices will be tolerated. Once this limit is reached, waiting ceases, and they face the consequences of their actions, known as "filling the measure." At this point, divine wrath may be unleashed upon them, leading to calamity. Until this threshold is reached, they may experience temporary success in their endeavors. This aligns with the notion that "For those who seek impurity, the gates are opened for them."[6] However, once the limit is surpassed, they face imminent destruction.

---

[5] Job. 36,10
[6] Yoma. 38b

It is crucial to recognize that Supernal providence meticulously oversees every detail, accounting for preceding and subsequent factors. In essence, it supervises every aspect while considering the interactions between all parts within the greater whole. From an individual's perspective, this encompasses their ancestors, descendants, contemporaries, community, and social circle. Following this comprehensive assessment, the individual is assigned their role within the divine service and test mentioned earlier, based on their designated responsibilities. However, it is essential to emphasize that this pertains to judgment in this world. In this context, one's role in divine service is determined by their state of being, which dictates the associated responsibilities. For the next world, however, individuals are judged solely based on their deeds and their true state, as the prophet proclaimed, "A son does not die for the sin of the father."[7] This distinction is essential because if a person merits wealth and abundance by divine decree, their descendants may be born into similar affluence.

Additionally, it is possible that due to their forebear's merit, a person may experience favorable or unfavorable circumstances at various points in their life. Similarly, salvation or adversity may befall them as a result of their descendants' destinies. Furthermore, depending on their geographic location and social environment, they may experience worldly fortunes or misfortunes.

---

[7] Ezechiel 18,20

Apart from individual judgment, there is another layer of divine providence concerning the righteous and their role in benefiting their generation or the entire world. This is rooted in the two aspects of providence we previously discussed: personal and general. The supernal wisdom foresaw the need for some individuals to assist others within the collective community mentioned earlier. It recognized the value of allowing not only those who attain completeness through their own merit but also those who achieve it through dependency on another's merit to partake in the blessings of completeness and be included in that collective.

However, those who rely on the merits of others will occupy a lower level within the collective, as they are dependent on their peers. They may not attain the highest level of perfection but will not be entirely excluded from it. They are considered worthy of enjoying completeness, although it is through their association with those who have reached a higher level. These individuals who benefit both themselves and others will hold prominent positions within the collective, assuming leadership roles, while those dependent on them will be subordinate, relying on their guidance.

To accommodate this significant rectification, people were initially bound to one another, as the sages declared, "All Jews are responsible for one another."[8] This interconnectedness fosters a sense of shared responsibility, whereby individuals become responsible not only for their own actions but also for

---

[8] Chevouot, 39a

the sins of others. By embracing this collective responsibility, they can affect positive change through their own merits and help elevate others.

Following this principle, it was arranged that righteous individuals might experience trials and suffering, ultimately atoning for the sins of their generation. It is incumbent upon the righteous to accept this suffering willingly, just as they would accept any personal suffering. Through this selfless act, they benefit their generation, acting as intermediaries of atonement and positioning themselves among the foremost in the collective destined for the world to come.

In the same category, there exists an even higher level of suffering. This occurs when a righteous individual endures suffering on behalf of their generation, who may be deserving of severe punishment and near destruction. By enduring this suffering, they atone for the sins of their generation and save them from temporal calamity while also securing benefits for them in the world to come. However, there is yet another form of suffering designated for the most righteous, those who have already achieved personal perfection. Their suffering serves a broader purpose, contributing to the general providential plan and its ultimate goal of achieving perfection.

This intricate system operates on the premise that suffering, both individual and communal, plays a pivotal role in clarifying and progressively eliminating contamination within both individuals and the world. Sins multiply this contamination, fortifying it within humanity and the world at large. This contamination, in turn, leads to the concealment of divine light, resulting in layer upon layer of obscurity. To counteract this, suffering—both on an individual and collective scale—serves to purify and remove contamination from the entirety of creation. Through the suffering of the righteous, the world advances incrementally toward perfection.

In guiding worldly matters, another fundamental principle emerges: the Supreme wisdom has ordained the increase of salvation. It is believed that a single soul can reincarnate several times in different bodies. Through these incarnations, the soul has the opportunity to rectify what was spoiled in a previous life or to complete unfinished tasks. However, at the culmination of these incarnations, the soul's ultimate judgment will be based on its experiences and states in each life.

Circumstances specific to a reincarnated soul may arise, influenced by its actions in past lives. Accordingly, a state will be assigned to that person in the world. The burden and judgment placed upon each individual will be meticulously tailored to their unique situation, ensuring no one is unfairly burdened in the afterlife with sins not truly their own. Each person's earthly responsibilities and trials are determined by the Supreme wisdom, and their actions are judged accordingly.

The process of reincarnation involves numerous specific aspects. A person's judgment will consider both their current life and past reincarnations, ensuring a fair and righteous outcome. As it is said, 'The Rock, His work is perfect, for all His ways are justice.'[9] The breadth of creation is such that no knowledge can fully grasp His thoughts and the depth of His counsel. We understand, as with other principles, that reincarnation is one of the drivers of human experiences in this world, governed by righteous laws and judgments preordained for the fulfillment of this grand design.

As we have explained, human experiences in this world are shaped by diverse and changing causes, whether for the good or for the beneficiary. Not every event stems from all these causes; rather, each human experience is drawn from specific causes. The Supreme wisdom, ever-knowledgeable and vigilant over the entire creation, considers all aspects in its profound counsel and thus orchestrates the world in every detail.

It is impossible for these causes to consistently yield identical outcomes, as they often contradict each other. For instance, a person might inherit wealth due to ancestral merit but face poverty due to their own actions. Even individual deeds can lead to differing outcomes: one deed might bring fortune, while another results in its absence.

Nevertheless, the Supreme Wisdom leans towards the favorable, orchestrating circumstances of various natures for each person, based on different causes. No event will occur to a person without aligning with one of these causes. Understanding the general principles of these matters and their

---

[9] Devarim. 32,4

types reveals much, though knowing every detail remains beyond human reach.

It is essential to understand that human experiences comprise two categories: ultimate and intermediate cases. Ultimate cases are those decreed for a person, aligning with one of the aforementioned causes. Intermediate cases occur to lead to another, more suitable event. An example is the saying, 'I will thank You, Lord, for You were angry with me,'[10] interpreted as a person whose cow broke its leg, fell, and revealed a hidden treasure.

Alternatively, a person may avoid a destined misfortune, such as missing a doomed ship due to a delay. These intermediate events might serve the person's needs or those of another, bringing about benefit or harm. The Supreme wisdom, in its assessments, considers these intermediates, ensuring all is resolved with the utmost precision for the greater good.

---

[10] Isaie. 12,1

Chapter 4 - Israel and the Nations of the World

A significant aspect of His governance involves Israel and the nations of the world. While these entities might seem equal in terms of human nature, they are profoundly distinct in the realm of Torah, akin to entirely different species. We aim to explore and elucidate the similarities and differences between them.

Adam Harishon, before his transgression, was in a state vastly superior to the current condition of mankind, a point we have previously addressed. The level of humanity in that era was exceptionally high, suitable for the lofty, eternal elevation we have mentioned. Without his sin, Adam would have continued to ascend, reaching higher and higher levels. In that exemplary state, it was appropriate for him to procreate, with the number and nature of his offspring being determined by Divine wisdom, ensuring their alignment with His goodness. These offspring would have shared in this divine delight. The planned offspring were not only conceived by Him but also categorized into distinct levels, including primary and secondary ones, roots, and branches, each following a specific sequence reminiscent of trees and their branches. The precise number of these trees and branches was also carefully considered. However, Adam's sin led to a steep decline in his status, introducing significant darkness and confusion into his being. Consequently, humanity collectively fell from its original high level to a much lower one, unfit for the originally intended elevation. This left humanity capable of producing offspring only at this reduced level. Yet, the potential for reaching the true essence of the human species, higher than its corrupted state, was not entirely lost. Adam Harishon remained on this lower level, with the potential to ascend back to the higher level.

The Master of the universe granted the offspring present at that time the choice to strengthen themselves and strive for elevation from their lowly state to the higher, supernal level. He allocated a period for this effort, as deemed appropriate by His supreme wisdom—a principle that applies to us in our quest for completeness and attaining a higher level in the collective future.

It was seen fit by the Supreme wisdom to segment this endeavor into two phases: initial efforts for the roots among the offspring, followed by efforts for their branches. This was necessary as humanity, in its entirety, needed to rectify its status due to the corruptions that had occurred. In terms of levels, it was appropriate to first rectify the roots and leaders of mankind's descendants. These roots and their branches would then maintain this corrected state, as branches invariably follow the root. This root-focused period spanned from Adam Harishon to the time of dispersion, marked by the dispersal of people after the construction of the Tower of Babel. Throughout this period, righteous figures like Enoch, Methuselah, Shem, and Ever continually sought truth for the masses, urging them towards self-correction.

When humanity reached a critical point at the time of dispersion, it was judged, in accordance with His justice, that the period focused on the roots should conclude. The aim was to establish what was appropriate at the root level based on all that had transpired up to that point. Observing all humans, He discerned the levels suitable for each individual based on their actions.

Accordingly, they were established at the root level as mentioned. As per their establishment, it was decreed that they would produce offspring corresponding to that root level. These beings were then recognized as established species in the world, each with its own laws and nature, similar to other species in creation. They were endowed with the capacity to reproduce according to their nature and level. By a supreme judgment, it was determined that they were to remain at the low level reached by Adam Harishon and his descendants due to the sin, not ascending beyond it. Abraham was the sole exception, chosen for his deeds, elevated, and established as a noble, lofty tree at the level of humanity's supernal aspect. He was granted the ability to produce offspring according to his nature. Consequently, the world was divided into seventy nations, each at a distinct level, but all embodying humanity's lower aspect, while Israel represented its higher aspect. Following this development, the focus shifted from roots to branches, initiating a new cycle.

In an act of abundant kindness, He allowed even the branches of other nations to uproot themselves from their original root and join the lineage of our father Abraham, should they choose to do so. This is why Abraham was made a father to converts, as God promised him, "And all the families of earth will be blessed through you."[11] However, should they choose not to pursue this path, they would remain under their original tree, according to their innate nature.

It is important to recognize that just as all of humanity is divided into original trees and their branches, so too is each individual tree distinguished by its primary branches, from which all other details branch out and subdivide. The primary branches of our tree, that of our father Abraham, are inclusive, represented by the six hundred thousand who left Egypt. From these individuals, the Jewish nation was formed. The Land of Israel was allocated among them. Everyone who descended from them is considered a part of these primary branches. The Torah was given specifically to this group, and thus this tree was considered to stand independently.

God extended a significant kindness to all nations by postponing their judgment until the giving of the Torah. He then offered the Torah to all nations, giving them the opportunity to accept it. Had they accepted it, they would have had the chance to rise from their low level. However, since they declined, their fate was sealed, and the gateway to elevation was permanently closed to them. The only option remaining for individuals from these nations is to voluntarily convert and join under our tree of Abraham.

---

[11] Bereshit. 12,3

The decree concerning these nations was not aimed at their destruction but to maintain them at the lower level mentioned earlier, a level of humanity that would not have existed if Adam Harishon had not sinned. It was his sin that brought this level into existence. Despite their lower status, these nations still possess a semblance of humanity. Accordingly, God wished for them to have something akin to what is fitting for true humanity. They have souls similar to those of Israel, albeit at a lower level. They are also given commandments, the Noahide commandments, through which they can achieve physical and spiritual success appropriate to their level. These provisions were pre-arranged from the beginning of creation, prepared in case humanity fell into sin, just like all other potential detriments and punishments.

In the world to come, there will be no nations other than Israel. The souls of the pious from other nations will be granted a form of existence that is subordinate to Israel, akin to how a garment is subordinate to a person wearing it. In this state, they will attain a certain degree of good, for it is not in their nature to achieve more than this.

When the world was divided in this way, God appointed seventy angels from the angelic class to oversee these nations. These angels contemplate and supervise their assigned nations. While God exercises general providence over these nations, the ministering angels provide detailed oversight with the authority granted to them by the Master of the universe. This arrangement does not imply a lack of knowledge on God's part regarding the details of these nations; everything is visible and revealed before Him. Rather, it means that He does not directly oversee and emanate to their details. This concept will be further explained in subsequent discussions, God willing.

In the divine scheme, God has intricately linked the rectification and elevation of the entire creation to the deeds of Israel. His providence, in this context, is made subordinate to their actions, determining whether to illuminate and emanate or to conceal Himself from them. In contrast, the actions of other nations do not directly influence God's revelation or concealment. Instead, these nations experience the consequences of their deeds internally, either benefiting or suffering physically and spiritually, and in doing so, they either strengthen or weaken their respective guiding angels.

Although God does not directly oversee the minutiae of the nations, He may choose to do so when it serves the needs of an individual or a group within the people of Israel. This intervention aligns with the nature of circumstantial occurrences, as we have elaborated in the preceding chapter

.

Chapter 5 – Providence

Until now, our discussion has centered on the laws of providence. We now turn our attention to the methods of providence, which fundamentally divide into two aspects: 1) His observation, and 2) His emanation.

In terms of His observation, it is well-established that His knowledge is all-encompassing, lacking nothing, be it past, present, or future. Every event, from the beginning of time to its end, has been foreseen by Him, leaving no aspect hidden from His view. The present, in all its intricacies, is fully revealed and known to Him, unobscured in any way. However, His role as an observer primarily involves judging and decreeing consequences upon these matters, actions that are bound by the timeframes He chooses to operate within. We will delve deeper into this aspect later, as God wills.

The matter of His emanation revolves around the implementation of His will, following a meticulously structured order and gradation of His own design. He has methodically organized His creations into a hierarchical sequence, descending in accordance with His divine plan. This specific order, intended for the existence and sustenance of creations, also governs their ongoing maintenance and the progression of their actions across all facets of their existence. Through this established hierarchy, He provides for each creation according to its inherent nature, infusing what is necessary for their respective functions and interactions.

His influence may be disseminated through an angel, which then imparts it to the angel below, continuing in this cascade down the levels until the final angel interacts with the physical world. Such interactions result in the establishment or modification of various matters, all aligned with His divine decree. It is vital to understand that the sustenance of any entity, at any level, is directly sourced from Him, as He is the sole maintainer of the creations and their interlinked chain, each in its unique nature.

When it comes to manifesting His influence in the physical realm, this process adheres to the specific order of beings and their interrelationships previously discussed, proceeding in accordance with the gradations mentioned.

God has designated specific natural guardians, tasked with unwaveringly upholding their assigned roles. These guardians adhere strictly to their duties unless a divine decree necessitates a deviation from the established order. For example, the angel responsible for trees diligently ensures their sustenance. However, should a divine decree command the winds to behave in a particular manner, the angel of winds will act upon the angel of trees, leading to the uprooting of trees through the force of the winds, as per the divine command.

This system is elaborate, featuring multiple levels of gradation and abundant details. Angelic guardians oversee the natural physical world, ensuring that all elements adhere to their natural laws. Above them, ministers of divine decrees guide the nature angels, orchestrating events as per the divine will. The intricacies of this system are extensive, mirroring the profound and concealed aspects of His governance.

Despite this system's complexity, God's oversight extends over every facet of creation, from the highest echelons down to the minutest details, from the roots to the branches. His surveillance is constant, and His focus unwavering. He continuously guides creation towards a state of ultimate perfection, with this divine guidance manifesting uniquely for each individual. Some are drawn closer, others are kept at a distance; some are refined, while others remain untouched. Each entity receives the divine influence most appropriate for it, ensuring the establishment of creation on a foundation of completeness.

God, in His will, alters the natural order of creation as He pleases, performing miracles and wonders according to His wisdom and the needs of the created beings in specific contexts. The assertion that He established conditions with all of creation does not imply He will never effect change; indeed, He can and does transform anything, anytime He desires a complete transformation. The crucial point is that, at the time of creation, He revealed to all foundational elements of creation their purpose and ultimate destinies, including their eventual transformations and ultimate outcomes.

They came to understand and accept that everything was progressing towards a truly benevolent end. They embraced and celebrated this knowledge, as indicated by the statement, "All of creation was created with their knowledge."[12] When God revealed to them the realities of their existence, their laws, and the truth of their incarnations, He also foretold that miracles would occur for Israel or its righteous ones at necessary times for their perfection. This was communicated to the supernal roots.

Subsequently, based on this revelation, the matter descended through emanation and materialized physically as warranted in each case. Trustees were appointed over these matters, upholding them according to their natural laws. Whenever He wishes, He issues decrees upon these trustees, prompting them to deviate from their assigned roles. Matters thus deviate from their natural course following His decree. These decrees can manifest in various forms, such as a command from a king or a rebuke from an angered ruler, exemplified in the verse, "He rebuked the Sea of Reeds, and it dried up,"[13] and similar instances in various contexts.

---

[12] Houlin. 60a
[13] Tehilim. 106,9

Chapter 6 - The Order of Providence

The Lord, blessed be He, has decreed that His governance over the entire world should adhere to a structured order, akin to that of earthly kingdoms. This structure applies both to the judgment of actions of those endowed with free will, and to the renewal of the world and its inhabitants. The sages have drawn parallels, stating, "The heavenly kingdom resembles earthly kingdoms." This means that divine governance operates through courts and councils, each with its own procedures and protocols. To facilitate this, the Lord has established various spiritual courts at specific levels, each following a particular order. It is before these courts that all matters requiring judgment are presented. Furthermore, it is through the decrees issued by these courts that all things are upheld and maintained, as expressed by Daniel, "The word is pronounced by the decree of the angels..."[14]

Behold, He—blessed be His name—manifests Himself in all these divine councils, bestowing His emanation upon them, and establishing them upon the true nature of the matter, ensuring truthful judgment. In some councils, the Holy One, blessed be He, positions Himself as the head, as stated in the verse, "I saw God sitting on His throne, and all the heavenly host standing by

---

[14] Daniel. 4,14

Him, at His right and at His left."[15] The sages explain that some angels argue for merit while others for guilt. Daniel also refers to this, saying, "Until thrones were set up and the Ancient of Days sat... He sat in judgment, and books were opened."[16] However, the essence of the matter is as follows: the judgment of each individual is marked by great precision. Generally, for any individual, numerous arguments can be made from various causes, leading to a multitude of legal judgments. Similarly, each action a person takes has aspects that could be seen as meritorious or guilty, in many different ways. This is because all matters in the world are inherently complex, comprised of various elements and drawn in numerous ways.

Yet, all these true aspects are laid bare in the heavenly courts, revealed in their true form. Each angelic being in the court perceives one of these aspects according to its nature, until collectively, all aspects are revealed with nothing concealed. The matter is then weighed according to all these true aspects, and a fitting decree is issued. However, the final decision is made by the head of that particular court. If it is one of the courts where the Lord, blessed be He, chooses to sit as head, even though He sees all, He allows all the ministering angels before Him to present their arguments according to the aspects of the matter revealed to them in truth. He then finalizes the matter as is fitting, as stated.

---

[15] Kings. 22,19
[16] Daniel. 7,9

From this foundational understanding, it follows that the Holy One, blessed be He, does not judge the world based solely on His omniscience. Instead, He judges according to the systems He has established for this purpose. Part of this divine ordinance is that no matter is brought to judgment in any of these heavenly courts until it has first been presented before appointed overseers. These overseers are angelic beings, designated by God to observe all that transpires in the world. They bring their testimonies to the heavenly court, where the matters are then adjudicated. It is important to note that these proceedings do not stem from God's knowledge; He sees all eternally. Rather, this is the system He has decreed in His profound wisdom, and it is according to these systems that the world operates in truth. Biblical verses such as "God went down to see,"[17] "The sons of God came to stand before Him,"[18] "The eyes of God range over all the earth,"[19] and "Those whom God sent to patrol the earth," allude to these paths of providence and the systems He has ordained.

The angels appointed to oversee matters in the world and testify about them are referred to as "The eyes of God." When God, blessed be His name, reveals Himself in one of the courts to judge a matter, as in the case of the builders of the Tower of Babel when it says "God went down to see," the same process applies to any similar case. However, it is crucial to understand that while the systems of divine judgment may be compared to

---

[17] Bereshit. 11,5
[18] Job. 1,6
[19] Zacharie. 4,10

those of earthly kingdoms, the actual execution of matters is not precisely the same. In the physical realm, matters are conducted according to human understanding and ways, whereas in the spiritual realm, matters unfold according to divine wisdom and ways.

The Lord, blessed be He, has appointed the prosecutor, who is Satan, as described in the verse "The Satan came within them."[20] The Satan's role is to demand judgment in the courts, and when he makes his demands, the judges are stirred to judgment. Out of His attribute of goodness, blessed be He, God does not initiate judgment until the accuser brings his accusations, even though the sins of the sinner are plainly visible to Him. However, even for this, God has established laws and ordained systems, dictating how and when the accuser may bring his accusations. This is reflected in the sages' teachings, such as "Satan accuses at the time of danger,"[21] "Three things bring a man's sins to mind,"[22] and many other similar details.

For all these judicial matters, both general and specific, there are established laws and pathways, as decreed by His divine wisdom. These laws dictate the times of judgment and its various aspects. This is reflected in the sages' statements, such as "The world is judged in four periods," "The King enters first, preceded by the snorting of His wrath," "Grain stands in judgment twice," as well as the distinctions between before and after a decree is issued, among several other details

---

[20] Job. 1,6
[21] Gen. Rabba 91,12
[22] Berachot. 55a

Chapter 7 - The Influence of the Stars

We have previously established in Part I that all physical entities originate from separate forces. These entities are initially rooted in various ways within these forces, and subsequently, they need to be conveyed and manifested into the physical realm in their required forms. For this purpose, the celestial spheres and their stars were created. They enable the transfer of all matters, initially rooted in spirituality, down to the physical world, ensuring they materialize in the correct form. The number, hierarchy, and divisions of the stars were meticulously determined by supreme wisdom to facilitate this transfer. Through the stars, the power of existence is bestowed upon physical entities beneath them, transforming their state from their spiritual roots to their physical manifestations.

Furthermore, the Creator, blessed be He, has instilled another function in these stars. They govern the occurrence of random events and outcomes in the physical world. After these events are preordained in the spiritual realm, they are channeled through the stars to manifest physically in their predetermined forms. Life, wealth, wisdom, progeny, and other such matters are first established in their spiritual roots and then drawn down to their physical branches in the appropriate form through the stars. This process follows specific classifications, combinations, and incarnations predestined for them. All random occurrences in the physical realm are distributed among the stars, categorizing them into different types, with all physical entities placed under their dominion, influenced, and renewed according to the emanations from the constellations and their individual connections to them.

All humans are also subjected to this celestial order, receiving influences according to the emanations from the constellations. However, the influence of the stars can be overridden by a superior and supreme force. This is the basis for the saying, "There is no constellation for Israel,"[23] indicating that the power of divine decree and influence surpasses the influence of the constellations, resulting in outcomes determined by the higher influence rather than the stellar one.

Moreover, the laws governing the influence of the stars are finite and determined by supreme wisdom. Some aspects of these laws can be discerned through astronomical observations, providing astrologers with partial insights into future events. However, they cannot grasp the entirety of the celestial order, and their predictions are not always accurate. Additionally, as mentioned earlier, the influence of the stars can be nullified, further limiting the accuracy of astrological predictions. This is reflected in the saying, "cannot grasp the entirety" - indicating that the insights gained from the stars are not comprehensive

---

[23] Shabbat. 156a

Chapter 8 - Details of Providence

In His precise providence, the Almighty ensures that all aspects of divine governance and its methodologies are rooted in justice and adhere to the principles of law, as expressed in the phrases, "The rod of equity is the rod of your kingdom,"[24] and "A king establishes the land through justice."[25] We understand that the divine will is inherently benevolent, and His love for His creations is comparable to a father's love for his son. However, out of this love, it is appropriate for a father to discipline his son for the latter's ultimate benefit, as stated, "For as a man chastises his son, so God your Lord chastises you."[26] Thus, justice and law originate from love, and divine chastisement is not punitive but rather a paternal correction aimed at the well-being of the child. From this foundation, two outcomes arise: firstly, the chastisement is tempered with mercy, making it gentler; secondly, there are times when divine wisdom necessitates bypassing the law entirely in favor of mercy, as stated, "And I will show grace to whomever I show grace, and I will have mercy on whomever I have mercy."[27]

Since humanity has been granted free will, divine providence appears to be contingent upon human actions, rewarding or

---

[24] Psalms. 45,7
[25] Proverbes. 29,4
[26] Devarim. 8,5
[27] Shemot. 33,19

punishing individuals based on their deeds. However, in reality, the Almighty is not bound by any laws or external influences, and He acts according to His will. For the administration of justice, He chooses to operate within the framework of reward and punishment based on human actions. Yet, when divine wisdom deems it necessary to transcend the boundaries of justice, He exercises His sovereignty and omnipotence to forgive transgressions and rectify damages. Consequently, there are two types of divine providence: the providence of reward and punishment, and the providence of dominion and uniqueness. Both forms of providence reflect the Almighty's constant vigilance and care for His creations.

It is crucial to understand that divine emanation is twofold: it pertains to both the body and the soul. Regarding physical well-being, we have already discussed how divine emanation influences an individual's prosperity and health in this world.

As for the soul, divine emanation relates to intellectual and spiritual growth, as well as the closeness of an individual to the Almighty. A prosperous state in this world is characterized by wisdom, devotion to the Creator, clarity of truth, suppression of wickedness, rejection of deceit, and exclusive worship of the Almighty. In such a state, virtues prevail, vices are shunned, and tranquility abounds, free from troubles and harm. The Almighty reveals His glory in the world, delights in the actions of His creations, and His creations find joy and fulfillment in His presence. Conversely, a state of decline is marked by indulgence in desires, neglect of wisdom, scarce devotion, prevalence of falsehood, dominance of wickedness, and proliferation of idolatry. Virtues are scarce, vices are rampant, tranquility is absent, and troubles and harm are prevalent. In this state, the Almighty conceals His glory, the world operates as if left to chance and natural forces, and both the Creator and His creations find no joy in each other. The wicked prosper, while the righteous are oppressed. Divine emanation thus influences all aspects related to the body and the soul, shaping the state of the world and its inhabitants.

As previously explained in Part I, Chapter 4, the human condition in this world is inherently rooted in materiality and darkness, yet it is also graced with divine illumination, which bestows knowledge and intellect. Initially, humans possess limited knowledge, but as they mature, their understanding grows. The source of all existence and knowledge is the divine emanation, which varies according to the degree of divine illumination or concealment, as discussed in Part I, Chapter 4. This dichotomy between illumination and concealment is the foundation of all good and evil in the world.

Divine emanation, characterized by either illumination or concealment, follows the decrees of divine wisdom. Illumination brings prosperity, merit, and honor, while concealment results in deprivation, coarseness, and lowliness. Since the existence of beings and the providence they receive are complex and multifaceted, encompassing aspects of abundance and lack, merit and demerit, honor and lowliness, the divine emanation they receive must be a nuanced blend of illumination and concealment, tailored to their specific needs and destinies. This intricate interplay of divine forces shapes the existence and experiences of all beings.

When we observe the overarching conditions of the world from its inception, taking into account historical events and prophetic revelations, we discern a fourth level in the progression of humanity. This level can be likened to the life stages of an individual, from birth to maturity.

The first state is characterized by pervasive ignorance and darkness, with a profound absence of true knowledge about the Divine. This is a state of extreme imperfection, referred to by the sages as "two thousand years of chaos."

The second state, which is an improvement over the first, resembles our current era. We are fortunate to possess knowledge of God's existence and His perfection, and we have access to His Torah. However, we lack the presence of signs, wonders, and prophecy, and the true understanding that comes from the Holy Spirit is absent. Human intellect, acquired through personal effort, is significantly inferior to the divine wisdom bestowed through the Holy Spirit.

The third state, superior to the second, is akin to the era of the Holy Temple, marked by the presence of signs, wonders, and prophecy. However, this divine emanation was limited to select individuals and was not as readily accessible due to various impediments.

The fourth and most elevated state, surpassing all previous states, aligns with the prophetic vision of the future. In this era, ignorance will be eradicated, the Holy Spirit will be abundantly poured upon all of humanity, and divine wisdom will be accessible without any hindrance. This state signifies the completion of humanity's spiritual development, ushering in an era of perpetual ascent and eternal bliss.

Examining the spiritual emanation further, we find that it is subject to specific limitations in terms of time, place, and other conditions. The Almighty has decreed that divine emanation should manifest in particular ways at certain times, and not in others, and similarly in specific places, and not in others. These intricacies are meticulously calibrated to optimize the well-being of creation. The sanctity of holy days and places is derived from this principle, as they are times and spaces where individuals can receive a greater share of divine emanation, leading to increased enlightenment, merit, and spiritual elevation.

Part 3 – The Soul and Prophecy

Summary of Part 3

Part 3 - Chapter 1

Man's divine soul subtly influences through dreams when detached somewhat during sleep. It maintains partial higher connection throughout life. Prophecy is an overwhelming, palpable grasp of divine revelation. The soul acts subtly, discernible through dreams when detached during sleep. Prophecy is a clear, tangible divine encounter.

Part 3 - Chapter 2

Man can transcend nature's boundaries using holy names to draw specific influences if worthy. Improper use is forbidden. Holy names compel angelic compliance within designated parameters. Holy names nullify select boundaries, enabling spiritual elevation in this life to channel influences. Proper use is limited. Holy names force angels to comply within set parameters.

Part 3 - Chapter 3

Prophecy causes overwhelming experience and comprehension beyond nature through mediated divine connection. Moshe's prophecy was unique.. Comprehension comes through the soul's clinging. Moshe's prophecy was unparalleled.

Chapter 1 - The Human Soul

As previously explained in Part I, Chapter 3, man possesses a unique characteristic not found in any other created being: the amalgamation of two distant and separate existences within him – the body and the soul. Man has an existential soul, as do all living creatures, which enables sensation and comprehension inherent in his nature. This soul, present in all living creatures, is a very subtle and distinct existence. It enters the seed post-conception, expands, and proceeds to construct the body according to the specific requirements of that species. As it develops, it also extends sensation and comprehension appropriate for that species. There is a notable variance in the comprehension abilities of different living creatures, with humans standing out due to their superior cognitive capabilities. This entire process unfolds naturally, following the laws of nature and contingent on the preparedness of the capacities serving the soul, varying across species.

In addition to these faculties, humans possess a range of powers within their soul, such as imagination, memory, intellect, and will. Each of these powers operates within known boundaries and in specific ways.

Humans also have a very distinct and supreme soul. Its primary purpose is to connect man to the supernal roots necessary for his deeds to produce significant impacts in the supernal forces.

This higher soul draws emanations for man from the supernal sources, channeling them to the existential soul, and from there to the body. It guides the lower soul, prompting necessary actions at every moment in a man's life, based on its connections with higher entities. This soul connects with the lower soul, which in turn connects with the most subtle part of the blood, forming a link between the body and both souls.

This connection subjects the higher soul to certain limitations and prevents it from associating with spiritual, separate existences as long as it remains connected to the body – essentially, throughout a person's lifetime. The body's deeds influence it, determining whether it connects to the Divine light or turns away to cling to impure forces. This depends on the individual's preparation for their destined perfection or their distance from it. The higher soul influences the lower soul, imprinting comprehension, thoughts, and will according to its orientation.

While we generally refer to it as one soul, it actually comprises many parts and levels, akin to multiple souls linked together in a chain. From these interconnected levels, the general higher soul is formed. Some parts of this soul may leave temporarily and return later, or new levels may be added and then depart, all without any visible impact on the body. The influence of these souls on the body is imperceptible; they neither enhance nor diminish vitality or sensation. Their role is to determine the true nature of man and his relationship with higher realms, based on his suitability for connection. This includes the concept of the additional soul that arrives on the holy Sabbath and departs at its conclusion, a process unfelt by the body. The general parts of the soul are divided into five levels: Nefesh, Ruach, Neshamah, Chayah, and Yechidah.

Despite its connections to the body, this higher soul has specific events suited to its nature, maintaining some connection with the spiritual realm. This does not translate into perceivable or recognizable intellect and thought in man, except occasionally and minimally. This is what the sages meant when they said, "Even though he does not see, his Mazal (constellation) sees."[28] The implication is that the matter reaches the higher soul but does not fully extend into conscious thought and intellect, resulting in only a slight arousal.

The Supreme wisdom has delineated time into two distinct segments: a period for the activities of men, and a period for their rest, identified as day and night. The daytime is reserved for activity, while the nighttime is meant for rest. Inherent in the nature of living creatures is the propensity to sleep, affording both their bodies and spirits a respite from their exertions.

This period of rest facilitates the rejuvenation of all their physical and mental faculties, enabling them to resume their tasks in the morning with renewed vigor. During sleep, an individual's faculties are subdued, their sensations are soothed, and their cognitive abilities enter a state of calm and repose.

---

[28] Meguila. 7a

The sole faculty that remains active is the imagination, which conjures images based on residual impressions from the waking hours, as well as influences from vapors and fumes ascending to the brain, originating from natural bodily processes or ingested food. This phenomenon underlies the dreams experienced by all individuals.

Additionally, the Creator has ordained that the higher soul, as previously discussed, should partially disengage from its physical ties during sleep. Specific components of the soul, extending up to the level of ruach, are meant to ascend and detach from the body, leaving only the nefesh in conjunction with the lower soul. These disengaged soul components then interact with the spiritual realm, as angels who oversee natural phenomenon, or malevolent angels as demons, contingent upon various factors.

Occasionally, the insights gained during these interactions filter down to the lower soul, prompting the imagination to generate images. The veracity of these insights can vary, being contingent upon the nature of the intermediary through which they were acquired. This information subsequently reaches the imagination, where it is visualized, at times with clarity, and at other times with confusion due to the distorted images stemming from the vapors. Through this mechanism, individuals can receive forewarnings or revelations pertaining to future events.

This process unfolds in accordance with divine decree, wherein knowledge is conveyed to the soul via one of the spiritual forces, and subsequently visualized in the imagination, either obscurely or distinctly, as determined by the supreme wisdom. This concept is encapsulated in the phrase, "In a dream, a night vision...then He opens men's ears."[29] Consequently, dreams are predominantly visualizations crafted by the imagination, either autonomously or under the influence of the soul's experiences.

The orchestrator in all these scenarios is one of the spiritual forces that communicates with the soul, translating this information into images within the imagination. If the force is divine, the information is truthful; if it originates from adversarial forces, the information is deceptive. All dreams incorporate a mixture of distorted images from the imagination, as expressed in the adage, "It is impossible to dream without vain things."[30] There also exist prophetic dreams, the nature of which will be elucidated separately, God willing.

[29] Job. 33,15
[30] Berakhot. 55a

Chapter 2 - Transcendental Forces and Sorcery

All creations originate from general separate forces, arranged in specific classes, from which the physical ones gradually emanate. The nature of evil forces, from which all evil emanates into the physical realms, has also been explained. The essence of the true existence of the created beings lies in the separate roots, with the physical realm being a continuation of what was rooted and established there. Everything was arranged and distributed according to what was deemed appropriate for the true existence of the creations and their purpose – what was meant to be in the roots and what was meant to be in the branches. The supreme wisdom drew everything into the chain of development, transforming their nature from form to form, until they were confined to their physical form.

Above all the physical stands the chain of their roots, ascending higher and higher up to the first forces. Each force remains in its place, sustained at its level and within its boundaries as imprinted by the Creator, never leaving them. All the roots influence their branches according to the chain of development, without ever deviating from their natural boundaries.

However, the Supreme wisdom decreed that the forces operating in the physical realm should also have the ability to act outside the order of development. This means that they can perform physical actions related to their nature, not the nature of the physical, altering the physical from its constant nature. The Creator endowed man with the ability to utilize creations in this way, just as He enabled him to use them naturally. This means that just as natural use is not entirely subject to man's will, being limited to specific methods and boundaries (e.g., one can only cut with a knife, climb with a ladder, or push soft materials), the spiritual use of creations is also confined to known boundaries and specific methods, as deemed appropriate by the supreme wisdom.

The Creator has established that certain boundaries, which separate and distance man from the spiritual creations and their matters, can be nullified. This frees man from their constraints, elevating him above his physical state and granting him access to the spiritual while still in his mortal body. However, not all the boundaries of nature are meant to be nullified, but only specific ones, as deemed fitting and proper by the supreme wisdom for the overall purpose of guidance. These boundaries are nullified under measured conditions and in specific ways.

The wisdom of the Creator has provided means for man to achieve this goal, should he desire and strive for it. These means enable him to nullify the natural boundaries within himself and elevate himself to the aforementioned level. The entire process depends on what will be explained next.

It is important to understand that the sustenance of all creations, both in general and in particular, comes directly from the Blessed Lord. All creations and their orders, whether they be higher powers, spiritual creations, or physical entities, are sustained by their dependence on Him. He exists and reveals Himself to all His creations, influencing them in ways that are appropriate for sustaining their purpose. These influences are diverse, reflecting the variety of recipients and their differences. The existence of all beings depends on these influences, which are categorized and detailed according to their nature. When these influences are drawn upon, all the offspring born from them come into being, following the entire chain of creation as He has arranged it. Angels receive enlightenment from His Blessedness, which is revealed to them according to their capacity to receive. The higher beings influence the lower ones, and so on, down the entire chain of creation.

The Blessed One desired to be called by a name, allowing His creations to connect with Him, call upon Him, mention Him, and draw close to Him. For this purpose, He designated a special Name for His honor, stating "This is My Eternal Name"[31]. This is the Name by which He is called, reflecting His honor as He desired to be named. However, for all the specific details of His influences, He has different names. He decreed that when His creations mention His name, an illumination and influence would emanate from Him to them, as the verse states "In every place where My Name is mentioned I will come to you and bless you"[32]. The type of influence that emanates depends on the name used to call upon Him. The influence that emanates will

---

[31] Shemot. 3,15
[32] Shemot. 20,21

be of the same type as that which the Name represents in relation to Him, Blessed is He. The influence continues down the entire chain of creation, as previously explained.

However, the Supreme wisdom has set boundaries and specific conditions for this process. When the mention of His name is complete and aligns with these conditions, the specific influence will emanate, and the result will occur. Connecting to Him and clinging to Him is certainly required for the first matter, which involves mentioning His Blessed Name to draw influence from Him. The more one engages in this practice, the easier it becomes to achieve the desired goal. For the second matter, this condition is not necessary, although its presence assists if it is present. After it was established as an innate power of these Names that the angels would be compelled by their mention, they return to their natural state, allowing the user to operate them according to his will, provided he uses them appropriately.

However, it is clear that it is neither fitting nor proper for a common person to use the scepter of a king. On this matter, the Sages have stated "One who makes use of the crown perishes"[33]. Permission for this practice is granted only to those who are holy and close to Him, who cling to Him, and who use this power to sanctify His Blessed Name and fulfill His will in any way possible. Without this, even though the action will not be prevented from the one who uses them if he follows the proper methods, he will be punished for his audacity. As previously stated, the practice is not absolute and is limited to the

---

[33] Avot. 1,13

boundaries deemed fitting by the supreme wisdom. Even within these boundaries, His Blessed decree will prevent the outcome whenever He sees fit, when His wisdom determines that prevention is fitting and proper.

After the decree of His wisdom was that there would be good and evil in the world, the order was that evil would truly be found in all the levels it is possible to exist, and the work of man would be to prevent its control and action in all its ways and levels, until its matter is fully removed from creation. However, you see that the Blessed Master of the worlds, His true essence precludes any type of deficiency whatsoever, as explained in Part 1 Chapter 1, and only in creations can deficiencies and evils be found. Behold, the order was to create levels of good for the creations, and to create for them the opposite, which is the existence of what is possible for evil, and man comes with his service and removes from its matter and from the entire creation all evil completely, and establishes in it and in creation the good eternally.

Therefore, the order was that opposite every matter of good would be found a matter of evil, and this is what the verse states "This opposite that God made"[34]. Only in one matter does good exceed evil, for the root of good is His eternal and supernal perfection, while evil is nothing but a created thing to be annulled, and it only exists for as long as the aforementioned endeavor of man.

---

[34] Eccl. 7,14

According to this way, just as the Blessed One provided man a way to attain through it illumination and prophecy beyond the way of nature, so too was it necessary that for this great good, the opposite exist, which is that man be able to draw darkness and cloudiness and a spirit of impurity beyond the natural way, and this is the matter of the impurities of witchcraft and communicating with the dead, which the Torah has distanced us from.

Their matter is to draw, by means of mentions with known conditions, influences of impurity and contamination, which is the greatest distancing from Him, may He be blessed, which is the opposite of clinging to Him, literally. The matter extends from those evil forces that we mentioned in Part 1 Chapter 5, that it was decreed upon them by His Blessedness that they would be mentioned by names and by their mention a draw of impurity would emanate from them in known levels beyond the natural way, and similarly they would perform actions beyond natural actions through them, according to the actions that were given over to those operative forces to perform, and in those boundaries that were placed upon them.

Similarly, through demons, actions like these will be performed, according to what was given over to them as well to perform, and within the specific boundaries designated for them. Behold, to the same degree that they were given the ability to act, the Blessed Master decreed that the appointees over nature, who uphold the affairs of the world in their natural state, along with all the angels who bring the influences according to the ordered system, would retreat before them. About this the sages, may their memory be blessed, stated "Witches – who silence the heavenly entourage"[35].

However, this will only be to that extent and no more. Even within that same extent, they can certainly still be repelled by a mightier force than theirs, and their actions can be prevented by His Blessed decree. About this it states "There is none besides Him"[36] – even [against] witches. They explained this is for one whose merits are great, that from Heaven they will save him and repel those who wish to harm him, as explained in the Talmud: "Shmuel the Little is different, for his merits are many"[37].

---

[35] Hulin. 7b
[36] Devarim. 4,35
[37] Hulin 7b

Chapitre 3 - The Holy Spirit and Prophecy

The Creator has ingrained within human nature the capacity to understand and comprehend when one observes creation, contemplating what is revealed and investigating the unrevealed until full understanding is achieved. This is the path of natural comprehension. However, He has ordained a superior form of comprehension—emanated comprehension. This involves the transmission of knowledge directly from His Blessedness through specific means He has established. Upon receiving this influence, a person gains an unequivocal understanding of a matter in all its causes and effects, according to their capacity. This phenomenon is referred to as the holy spirit.

Through this process, one can grasp matters within the realm of natural comprehension with unparalleled clarity and precision, as previously explained. Furthermore, it enables the understanding of matters beyond the grasp of natural comprehension, including future events and hidden things.

Glimmer of the holy spirit – concealment: However, this phenomenon varies in degrees, influenced by the strength of the emanated flow, its timing, the manner of its reception, and the nature of the revealed knowledge. Despite these variations, the recipient will always perceive the revelation tangibly.

Nonetheless, there may be instances where the emanated flow subtly influences a person's heart, enlightening them about a matter in a manner similar to a spontaneous thought.

Beyond the holy spirit lies prophecy, a state where a person connects directly with the Blessed Creator, clinging to Him in a palpable manner. The individual feels this connection and comprehends the divine glory in a way that will be further elucidated. This realization is clear and tangible, free from any doubt, akin to the certainty one feels when perceiving a physical object. The essence of prophecy is this grasp of divine connection and understanding, achieved during one's lifetime, signifying immense spiritual perfection. Accompanying this state is a profound understanding of divine secrets, attained through emanated comprehension, with a clarity and intensity surpassing that of the Holy Spirit (Ruach Hakodesh), as will be discussed, G-d willing.

However, this connection is mediated, not direct. The prophet does not grasp the divine glory as one sees another person directly. Instead, intermediaries serve this purpose, functioning like a lens aiding vision, facilitating the divine encounter. The true object of this connection is the divine glory itself, though the nature of the connection varies with the intermediaries, similar to viewing through a microscope. Levels of proximity, clarity, and opacity of the lens are discernible in this process.

Upon the divine revelation and the emanation of His flow, the prophet experiences an overwhelming force, causing physical trembling and upheaval, a testament to the human body's inability to endure such spiritual revelation, especially of the divine glory. All senses and mental faculties cease independent function, suspended in the divine flow. The soul's connection results in comprehension beyond human capacity, as understanding now stems from the divine connection. What is comprehended in this state surpasses the inherent nature of the knowledge itself. This is the general nature of prophecy for all prophets, though specific levels vary, as previously discussed, G-d willing. Above all stands Moshe Rabbeinu, whose unique prophecy is attested to in the Torah, having known G-d face to face[38].

When God reveals Himself and bestows His influence upon the prophet, it overpowers the prophet with great force, and immediately his physicality and all limbs of his body shake and feel as if they are turning upside down, for this is the nature of physicality - it cannot bear spiritual revelation, let alone the revelation of God's glory. His senses are nullified, and even his mental faculties do not function at all independently, rather they all remain suspended in God and His emanating influence. Through the clinging of his soul, an existence of comprehension beyond all human comprehension is added to it, as it is comprehension in the aspect of his being bound with his Creator.

What he comprehends will thus be in a manner far more sublime than what can be grasped from it in and of itself. In this

---

[38] Devarim. 34,10

the prophet's power surpasses even one with divine inspiration in attaining knowledge, for he comprehends with a supernal comprehension beyond any humanly possible, which is comprehension in the aspect of being connected to the Creator. The revelation of God's glory is what will cause all that comes to the prophet in his prophecy. From it, by the imaginative power of the prophet's soul, matters will be imagined that are necessitated by the supernal revelation, not of his own accord at all. From those imaginations, thought and comprehension will follow, engraved by the power of the revealed glory, and the matter will remain fixed in his intellect, so that even when he returns to his human state, the knowledge will remain in his clear consciousness.

This is the general concept of prophecy for all prophets, but there are many particular levels, as mentioned earlier, God-willing. Above all was the level of Moshe our teacher, peace be upon him, about whom the Torah testifies that no prophet like Moshe ever arose in Israel, whom God knew face to face.

Chapter 4 – The Prophetic Experience

When a prophet reaches the full stature of prophecy, he will perceive everything that is accessible to him with clear understanding and complete knowledge. This means that, even though, as we mentioned in the previous chapter, imaginations precede and then thoughts follow in the ways we mentioned, upon reaching the clarity of his prophecy, he will truly attain his status as a prophet. This means he is connected to the Divine and the Divine reveals and works through him in all those actions. He will perceive that the imaginations which are depicted in him are prophetic, inspired by the divine influence flowing upon him, establishing in him the knowledge of the matter determined by this influence, leaving no doubt in his prophecy or its aspects, neither the preceding nor the subsequent ones.

What you need to know is that a prophet does not reach the highest level all at once, but ascends step by step until he achieves complete prophecy. There is a learning process, just like in all other wisdoms and crafts, where a person ascends through levels until he stands on solid ground. This is the matter of the 'sons of the prophets,' who stood before the prophet to learn the ways of prophecy as necessary.

It is possible that a revelation from the Divine comes to a person and he does not recognize it as the prophet does, but considers it to come from the perceptible world, until the prophetic influence strengthens over him and then he recognizes the matter as it truly is. This was the case with the calling of the Lord to Samuel, who initially did not prophesy and the influence did not flow upon him, but only a voice like a perceptible sound was revealed to him, and he did not grasp more than this. But later the influence flowed upon him and he recognized and grasped the prophecy and its ways. Likewise, the vision of the burning bush to Moshe; at first, it was revealed to him only as perceptible and he saw the bush burning with fire, and God called him as his father's voice, but later the influence flowed upon him and he grasped the true prophecy.

However, those learning prophecy will learn known matters, what the supreme influence draws upon them, eliminating the physical body's impediments, and attracting the revelation of His light and cleaving to Him. Generally, the focus is on intentions and recitations of the holy names, and those immersed in praises will be refined with these names in the ways of combinations, and so on. As they merit through their deeds, purify themselves and proceed through these matters, so they will draw closer to the Blessed One, and the influence will begin to flow upon them and they will achieve understandings after understandings until they reach prophecy.

The distinguished prophet who already knows the ways of prophecy correctly, will teach each one according to his preparation what to do to achieve the desired end. Similarly, when revelations begin upon them, the prophet will teach them according to the nature of the revealed matter, and what is still lacking for them from the goal they seek. They will need a teacher and a guide until they stand firmly in the completeness of prophecy. For even though revelations and influences begin upon them, they will not immediately reach the end of the matter but will need much guidance to reach the end correctly, each according to his level and preparation.

Even after attaining the level of prophecy, prophets differ from one another in level and degree, both in quantity and quality. This means that some will prophesy many times, and some will prophesy only a few. Also, in the quality of the prophecy itself, some will achieve a great attachment to the Divine and understand very great concepts, while others' attachment and understanding will not be as great. However, all prophets will have a noticeable attachment to the Divine, and a clear revelation from Him to them, so clear that they will not doubt it. However, in the attachment itself, in the revelation and understanding, the many levels of distinction will be recognized.

Among the things that come to prophets is their being sent on missions by the Divine. This is not the essence of prophecy and is not at all necessary for a prophet to be sent to others. The essence of prophecy, as we have explained, is attachment to the Divine and His revelation to the prophet, accompanied by the knowledge and understandings that follow. Often, prophets are sent to others on missions. This can happen to a distinguished prophet, very skilled in the ways of prophecy and knowing them well. It can also happen to one who is not so skilled and learned in this, and in this respect, prophets can make mistakes, not in what they prophesy, but in what they do of their own accord, and not fulfilling their mission properly and being punished. Like the prophet of Jeroboam who transgressed his own words, which resulted from his lack of precision in the ways of prophecy, as our Sages of blessed memory discussed in the Talmud[39].

Furthermore, it is possible for a prophet among the prophets to grasp a true matter in his prophecy, but not to grasp all the true matters included in it. For example, the prophecy of Jonah son of Amittai who was told, 'And Nineveh shall be overturned,' which included two true meanings, one – the punishment that was prepared for them according to their sin, and the second – what was foreseen before Him, that they would turn from evil to good. However, if only the matter of punishment had truly been included in the speech, when God repented of the evil, He would have revealed the matter to the prophets and specifically to Jonah, as a new decree other than the first would have been renewed upon them.

However, since God included both meanings in the first speech, there was no need for a new decree upon them, but the speech was fulfilled in the second understanding and not the first. Yet Jonah initially grasped only the first understanding and not the second, and this is what our Sages of blessed memory said, 'Jonah was the one who did not discern.'[40]

---

[39] Sanhedrin 89b
[40] Sanhédrin 89b

Indeed, you need to know that in the prophecy of the prophets, two distinctions are made: the first, the matter, and the second, the words and expressions. This is because a prophet may grasp a matter from among the matters, and it is not limited to words, but the prophet will express it in words as he wishes. Some may grasp a matter that is also limited in words, like the prophecies of Isaiah, Jeremiah, and other written prophets for generations, where their words in prophecy are limited to include many matters as one.

Even in this, the expression will change according to the prophet's own preparation and ways, and will also conform to the nature of his language and manner of speaking. Often, prophets are given to perform actions along with their prophecies, such as Jeremiah's belt, Ezekiel's yoke and brick, and many such. The point was that through these actions, they would stimulate powers from the higher realms, necessary according to the true nature of the matter upon which the prophecy was in all its aspects, and from then on, they would be opportunely and providentially brought to actualize the matter at the appropriate time.

Furthermore, you need to know that the true and precise title of prophet is fitting only for one who has already achieved prophecy in its fullness and has clarified for himself that he truly prophesies from the Divine, and so on. One who has reached this will have no doubt in his prophecy at all, and will not err in his prophecy. However, in a broader sense, this title can also be attributed to one who begins to achieve prophetic understandings and has received a revelation beyond the human realm. However, one who has only achieved these understandings is not yet secure in his matter, and it is possible for him to err, like the prophets of Ahab, as we will explain later, God willing. Indeed, those who know the ways of prophecy well, know all this accurately, know these potential pitfalls, recognize their signs, and the way to be saved from them until reaching the truth of prophecy. These were the teachers of the students, as mentioned, saving them from errors and establishing them in the truth.

However, the main point of this matter is what was said in Part 1, Chapter 5, about those forces of impurity that exist in the world and act according to what is decreed in their nature and given into their hands. Indeed, they have the power to deceive a person, influencing him in ways similar to the true ways of prophecy, revealing to him true and false matters, and inventing some wonderful matters, as the scripture explicitly says about the false prophet, 'He gives you a sign or a wonder, and the sign or the wonder comes to pass.'[41]

This can happen to a person unwillingly, or it can happen willingly. That is, this occurrence can happen to him without his striving for it, or even striving against it, and it comes to him because his actions and efforts are not complete. Or it can come to one who desires it in his wickedness and strives to achieve it, that is, he follows these forces and strives to cling to them willingly to achieve from them what he desires, that is, they

---

[41] Devarim. 13,2

reveal to him matters as mentioned, with which he presents himself before people as a prophet and misleads them as he desires or gains honor in their eyes.

Of this kind were the prophets of Baal and Asherah, who strove for this until they clung to these forces, attaining knowledge of certain things with which they deceived those who believed in them, and likewise they produced wonders with this power as a sign of their prophecy, as mentioned. Indeed, they themselves knew that this was from the impurity they had chosen, and did not consider themselves prophets, but did so out of the wickedness of their hearts.

Yet, even for one who did not strive for this, it was possible that this could occur, as mentioned, and therefore those striving for prophecy needed a distinguished teacher to teach them as mentioned, and through him, they were saved. All this, until they reached the true level of prophecy, for once they reached it, they saw the great difference and recognized it, and it was no longer possible for them to be in doubt about it at all, as mentioned.

The incident involving Ahab's prophets and the deceptive spirit can be traced back to this principle. Due to Ahab's actions, a divine decree determined that he would meet his end in Ramoth Gilead. It was crucial for him to face a strong temptation, compelling him to proceed to war without hesitation, despite clear signs advising against it. This played out when Jehoshaphat requested divine guidance, and the false prophets' assurances were insufficient for him, as all these events unfolded under divine scrutiny.

In the Heavenly Court, as the judgment was being deliberated, both accusers and defenders presented their cases, and various means of enticement were considered. The deceptive spirit emerged as the most suitable option. The false prophets, in Ahab's presence, would perform actions and engage in practices associated with prophecy, solely aiming to channel the impure spirit mentioned earlier.

Their intention was not to seek enlightenment from the Divine, but to deceive the king and make him believe they were receiving divine messages. In Ahab's presence, they endeavored to draw upon this impure revelation, and indeed, the revelation they sought was bestowed upon them. This performance in front of the king was meant to bolster his trust in them, fulfilling the biblical verse, "And all the prophets prophesied before them."[42]

The impure prophecy they received contained the message, "Go up and succeed, and G-d will deliver the king into your hand," spoken through them by the deceptive spirit. The prophets themselves were not mistaken about their practices; they were fully aware of their engagement with impurity. It was Ahab who misinterpreted their actions and was misled, to the point of disregarding Micaiah's words due to his unwavering faith in his false prophets.

---

[42] Kings. 22,10

Zechariah ben Kena'ana, however, went a step further than the other prophets. While they simply relayed the messages received from the impure spirit, Zechariah mimicked the behavior of true prophets. He genuinely believed in the revelation, convinced it was a true message from the Divine, and boldly proclaimed, "So said the L-rd." He failed to accurately learn the ways of true prophecy and could not discern between falsehood and truth.

The Sages, may their memory be blessed, commented on this, noting that he spoke of things he did not hear and was misled by the spirit of Navot. They also emphasized the importance of precision in prophecy, as Jehoshaphat had warned, highlighting that two prophets do not share the same prophetic style.

In reality, the prophets experienced something unusual at that time, a deviation from their usual practices, leading Zechariah to mistakenly believe he was receiving a true prophecy, even though their efforts were solely directed towards impurity. This extraordinary event was a divine occurrence, and it is crucial to understand this well.

Chapter 5 - The Difference Between All the Prophets and Moshe

Generally, prophecy is categorized into two levels: one encompasses all prophets except Moshe, and the other pertains solely to Moshe. This distinction, established by God Himself, is elucidated in scripture: 'If there be a prophet among you, I, the Lord, will make myself known unto him in a vision, speak unto him in a dream. Not so with my servant Moshe.'[43]

Except for Moshe, the common experience for all prophets involves receiving prophecy through visions or dreams. As stated, 'I will make myself known unto him in a vision, speak unto him in a dream.' This implies that God employs the natural phenomenon of dreaming as a conduit for conveying prophecy. The point is not that prophecy and dreaming are identical, but rather that dreaming serves as an appropriate medium for transferring prophecy, infused with divine wisdom. The saying, 'A dream is one-sixtieth of prophecy,' reflects its capacity to convey narratives and insights beyond ordinary human comprehension, as previously mentioned.

As prophetic influence intensifies, the prophet becomes detached from his sensory and conscious self, akin to being asleep. His mindset mirrors that of a person asleep and dreaming, at which point prophecy is imparted. This can occur

---

[43] Bamidbar. 12,6

while the prophet is awake, as earlier indicated, or during sleep in a nocturnal dream. Regardless, prophecy is received only once he has disengaged from his senses and entered a state of slumber. This state might be brief, with the prophet swiftly reverting to his usual self, yet during his prophetic episode, he is momentarily withdrawn from normal perception and immersed in transitory slumber.

The vision of the prophets doesn't resemble viewing through a clear lens where subjects are distinct. Their perception is more akin to seeing through multiple lenses with the image transitioning between them. The observed subject is unambiguously singular, and its movements are discernible through these lenses, albeit not in a straightforward manner. Furthermore, their vision is comparable to peering through a somewhat opaque lens, obstructing a clear view of the subject. Consequently, they are unable to discern the glory with clarity, despite what they indeed witness being His glory, about which they hold no doubt.

Even within this, varying degrees of clarity and distinctions exist among prophets, with some possessing clearer 'lenses' and thus achieving sharper perception. Nevertheless, a prophet who fully perceives all this truly grasps the essence of the revelation, recognizing that the revealed and known entity is the Creator. They understand the nature and secrets of this 'lens' and genuinely and vividly capture the insights imparted to them, as detailed in Chapter 3. As the glory is revealed through these image transitions, knowledge and insights are also conveyed to them through riddles, parables, and in dream-like manners, serving as mediums for prophecy.

However, the nature of Moshe's prophecy stands above all this. Firstly, he did not need to withdraw from his sensory and conscious state and did not experience dreams. His prophecy was granted while he remained in his normal condition, as said about him, 'With him will I speak mouth to mouth.'[44] His perception was as lucid as someone seeing through a single, clear lens, and his knowledge was imparted directly, not through riddles, as it is said, 'And the similitude of the Lord shall he behold.'

Nevertheless, even for Moshe, the glory was revealed to the extent that he could apprehend it, akin to an image reflected in a mirror, recognizing that it is impossible for a human to fully grasp the Creator. Yet, he clearly perceived the entire image, as if through a clear, luminous lens without obstruction. This is exemplified by 'And the similitude of the Lord shall he behold,' where he distinctly saw the depicted image, the similitude. Unlike other prophets, Moshe could fully comprehend this image. From it, he gleaned profound and crystal-clear understanding, surpassing that of any other prophet.

Another distinction between Moshe and other prophets lies in their ability to prophesy. The others could not prophesy at will, only when God chose to bestow His influence upon them. In contrast, Moshe could initiate communication with God and

---

[44] Bamidbar. 12,8

receive revelation as required. Furthermore, while other prophets were privy only to specific matters chosen by the Lord for revelation, Moshe was endowed with the privilege of having the entire order of creation unveiled to him, empowered to explore and inquire into all. He was entrusted with all the keys ever given to a human, as stated, 'Faithful in all my house,'[45] and, 'I will make all my goodness pass before you.'[46]

Just as all prophets perceived the image presented to them from the glory and understood the secret and significance of the image – the rationale for its portrayal, its transmission, and its purpose – they also grasped the fundamental truth that, in reality, there is no image in God. The depicted image is merely a construct for the prophet's eyes, crafted by God's will for a specific purpose. This is conveyed to Israel as, 'You saw no manner of similitude on the day that the Lord spoke to you,' and similarly, 'For you saw no manner of similitude.'[47] They comprehended both aspects: first, that God's true existence is utterly devoid of any image or form, and second, following this realization, they were also shown a prophetic image, as stated, 'And they saw the God of Israel,'[48] etc. Hence, the Sages termed it 'A vision of speech,' not an actual vision of the glory, but a vision formed through the power of speech, resembling an image in a lens. This enabled them to grasp specific matters in the mysteries of His divinity, creation, and providence, as elucidated."

---

[45] Bamidbar. 12,7
[46] Shemot. 33,19
[47] Devvarim. 14,12
[48] Shemot. 24,10

Part 4 - Serving God

Summary of Part 4

Part 4 - Chapter 1

Divine service comprises Torah, prayer, and deeds to perfect man and rectify creation through clinging to God and shedding material bounds. It requires strengthening the soul and achieving self and cosmic perfection. The service aims for self and collective perfection by transcending physicality and bolstering intellect and soul. It has continual, daily, timely and circumstantial aspects.

Part 4 - Chapter 2

Torah draws divine influence; comprehension determines impact. Proper conditions and purity allow personal and collective transformation. No Torah study lacks influence but depth determines impact. Internalization requires proper intentionality and conduct. Comprehension rectifies self and universe.

Part 4 - Chapter 3

Love binds one to God. Awe refines physicality, amplifies the soul's radiance, lifting one closer to the Divine. Great awe grants constant connection. Love empowers and connects through joy and yearning. Awe invites enlightenment, purity and divine presence.

Part 4 - Chapter 4

Shema invokes reciprocal revelation of divine unity as creation is elevated through blessings affirming sovereignty. Shema affirms God's oneness in existence and dominion. Blessings elicit reciprocal revelation, drawing influence. Reciting Shema rectifies man's faculties and creation's aspects.

Part 4 - Chapter 5

Prayer draws near God before worldly endeavors. Bowing elicits compassion. Prayers connect creation and draw influence. Prayer precedes worldly efforts, ensuring proper orientation. Bowing invokes mercy. Prayers follow precise order to elevate creation and draw influence.

Part 4 - Chapter 6

Night empowers impurity countered by morning prayers. Donning Tefillin extends divine light. Prayers parallel offerings and times. Evil dominates at night, morning prayers counter its effects. Tefillin draws holiness. Prayers connect to Temple rituals. Sections align with spiritual realms.

Part 4 - Chapter 7

Holy days provide sanctity, detach from materialism. Festivals recreate past revelations through observances. Levels of observance reflect spiritual elevation. Shabbat detaches from materialism. Festivals commemorate past events. Observance levels match spiritual states. The goal is reexperiencing transcendence.

Part 4 - Chapter 8
Holidays link observances to commemorated occasions. Shofar overpowers judgment with mercy. Torah reading was instituted as spiritual rectification. Cyclical reading maintains constant connection. Rituals recreate spiritual occasions. Shofar arouses compassion.

Part 4 - Chapter 9
Blessings redirect physicality to divine service and perfection. Food blessings express thanks and sanctify enjoyment. Mitzvah blessings show gratitude and endearment. Blessings aim to serve God through materiality. Food blessings honor God and elevate enjoyment. Mitzvah blessings also express devotion.

Chapter 1 - The Parts of the Service

The fourth part of our discussion centers around the service, breaking it down into two main components: study and action. When we delve deeper into action, we find it can be further divided into four distinct categories: continual, daily, timely, and circumstantial.

The continual aspect encompasses the constant obligations one has, such as the cultivation of love and awe towards G-d. Daily obligations include practices that should be performed each day, such as prayer and the recitation of Shema, which have taken the place of the offerings made in the Temple in times past. Timely obligations refer to duties that arise during specific times or seasons, like Shabbatot and various Holidays. Finally, circumstantial obligations are those that arise due to particular life events or situations, including matters like ritual impurity, tithing, or the redemption of the firstborn. Each of these categories includes both commandments and prohibitions, encouraging a practice of turning away from evil and striving to do good.

The essence of all these practices, in a broader sense, has been previously explored in Part 1 Chapter 4. It revolves around turning towards G-d, seeking to draw nearer to Him through the paths He has laid out for us. This journey requires us to shed the burdens of physicality and worldly distractions, striving instead to draw closer to Him, eventually achieving a state of perfection through His perfection. This, as we have established, is the ultimate desire of G-d and the very purpose for which He created the world.

However, the specific practices and obligations we follow are determined by the divine decrees that outline the nature of humanity and the world, in all their complexities. There are prescribed ways for man to achieve self-perfection and contribute to the completion of the entire creation, all intricately connected in a grand, ordered chain of being. In the sections that follow, we will delve into some of the most pertinent and universally applicable aspects of these practices.

Chapter 2 - Torah Study

Torah study is an indispensable aspect of our journey towards perfection. Without knowledge of what is expected of us, action becomes impossible. Beyond its role as a prerequisite for action, Torah study serves a greater purpose in the perfection of man— a topic we touched upon briefly in Part 1 Chapter 4, but will now explore in greater detail.

Looking at Torah study through the lens of divine influences, we recognize that among all the influences that emanate from G-d to sustain His creation, there exists a supreme influence, unparalleled in its preciousness and sanctity. This influence represents the essence of true existence, the epitome of divine supremacy and glory. G-d has chosen to bind this sublime influence to the Torah, creating a connection that manifests through both verbalization and comprehension.

The Torah, encompassing the Five Books of the Pentateuch, the Prophets, and the Writings, serves as a conduit for this divine influence. When we recite its words or delve into its meanings, we draw this influence upon ourselves, provided we adhere to the prescribed boundaries and true intentions of the text. The influence varies in its intensity, depending on the level of engagement and understanding, but no act of Torah study is devoid of this divine gift, as long as it is approached with sincerity and correctness.

The deeper one's comprehension, the greater the divine influence they draw upon themselves. A basic understanding of the text's language cannot compare to grasping its true intent, just as a superficial interpretation pales in comparison to a more profound, analytical approach. Yet, in His kindness, God has ensured that every level of engagement with the Torah brings with it a share of this great and special influence, allowing all of Israel to benefit, each according to their level of understanding and effort.

Beyond the individual reward and spiritual elevation that comes with Torah study, there is also a communal and cosmic aspect to consider. Every portion of the Torah contributes to the rectification and completion of the entire creation. To serve God in a comprehensive manner, one must engage with all parts of the Torah, distributing their efforts to ensure that no aspect of creation is left untouched by the divine influence channeled through their study. The sages advise a balanced approach, dividing one's study time between Scripture, Mishnah, and Talmud, thereby encompassing all facets of the Torah. The exact distribution should be tailored to each individual's nature and circumstances, a topic explored in greater detail in the dedicated essay, "Derekh Etz Haim – Derekh Hokhma."

However, achieving a profound understanding and connection with the Torah necessitates an immersive and respectful approach. This is grounded in the belief that the Divine has intricately linked His unique influence to the Torah. Engaging with it through speech and comprehension allows this powerful influence to emanate, transforming both the individual and the collective. Absent this reverence, the Torah's words would be indistinguishable from mundane human speech, and its teachings would not transcend the intellectual to touch the soul.

Embracing the Torah demands a deep sense of awe, recognizing the sanctity of approaching the Divine. This involves cultivating humility, recognizing the discrepancy between our human limitations and the Divine exaltedness. Yet, this approach is not rooted in fear alone, but also in joy — a joy tempered with reverence, acknowledging the privilege of partaking in something so sacred.

The physical posture and manner of engagement are integral to this process. A casual or disrespectful demeanor, whether towards the Torah's words or its physical manifestations in books, is incongruent with the gravity of approaching the Divine. Upholding these conditions ensures that the study is authentic, allowing the Divine influence to permeate, enriching the individual and contributing to the broader cosmic rectification.

Conversely, neglecting these conditions diminishes the study's impact, reducing it to mere intellectual exercise. This is especially true for those whose actions are not aligned with the teachings of the Torah. Engaging with the Torah demands purity of action, as the Divine influence is not accessible to those entrenched in impurity and estrangement from the Divine. The sages warn against imparting the Torah to those unprepared, emphasizing the gravity of misusing something so sacred.

Yet, the sages also reveal a profound truth: the inherent sanctity of the Torah has the power to transform, even for those initially unworthy. Consistent engagement with the Torah creates a conduit for Divine influence, gradually steering the individual back towards righteousness. This transformative power is, however, contingent on the sincerity of engagement, excluding those who approach the Torah with mockery or distortion.

The extent of one's preparation and sanctification directly influences the impact of Torah study. The sages of earlier generations, exemplified by their profound reverence and preparation, drew an unparalleled level of Divine influence through their study, a phenomenon less evident in later generations. The story of Yonatan ben Uziel, while studying, birds that flew over him would combust, stands testament to the extraordinary power of Torah study when approached with the requisite sanctity.

Chapter 3 - Awe and Love of God

In Part 1, Chapter 4, we delved into the concepts of love and awe, highlighting their significance in fostering a close and devoted relationship between an individual and their Creator. We distinguished between true love and awe—love for His Name rather than for personal gain, and reverence for His grandeur instead of fear of punishment. Such awe propels a person from the shadows of physical existence, inviting the Divine Presence into their life. The depth of one's awe directly correlates with their level of purity and their ability to receive Divine inspiration.

Those who live in a state of constant awe are graced with an unceasing connection to the Divine Presence. Moshe Rabbenu exemplified this, as he treated awe as a basic component of his spiritual practice, which in turn granted him continuous divine inspiration. While this state may be challenging for others to achieve, the extent to which one can embrace it determines the strength of their purity and sanctity. This is particularly crucial during engagement with commandments or scholarly pursuits, as awe is a prerequisite for the successful completion of these spiritual endeavors.

Love serves as the binding force that connects an individual to their Creator, empowering them and adorning them with grandeur. It manifests as heartfelt joy and a soul's fervent yearning for the divine, leading one to dedicate their entire being to the sanctification of His Name and seeking His pleasure. These concepts have been thoroughly addressed in previous sections, and thus, do not require further elaboration here. Integral to this discussion are faith in the divine and acknowledgment of His unity, trust, and other related matters—all of which strengthen the bond between a person and their Blessed Creator, fostering a sense of holiness and enlightenment within them.

Chapter 4 - The Shema and Its Blessings

The matter of the oneness of His existence and the oneness of His dominion first emerges in the Shema, which centers on His oneness and the acceptance of the yoke of His kingdom. The Blessed Creator, according to His will, has brought various supernal and lower, spiritual and physical creations into existence. He has arranged them in diverse orders and ingrained in each a nature to perform actions, to cycle through numerous incarnations, and to operate in various ways according to the wisdom He has allotted to each.

However, He, may His Name be blessed, stands as the sole root and cause of them all. This concept is grasped through two aspects: the aspect of existence and the aspect of action. In terms of existence, as previously explained in Part 1, all existences depend on Him, may He be blessed, and are drawn according to His will. His existence, in contrast, is necessary and intrinsic, not contingent upon anything else. All other existences maintain their being only insofar as He, may He be blessed, wills and sustains them. In terms of action, even though creations have been endowed with a nature that grants them dominion over certain matters and the capacity to perform significant actions, the truth is that they possess no power or dominion aside from what the Creator has delegated to them. He remains the true Master, Ruler, and Omnipotent, with everything they do being a manifestation of the power He has granted them. He holds authority over them to increase or decrease their capabilities according to His will at any given time.

The complexity of this matter lies in the fact that, as per the orders His wisdom has set for the betterment of creations, detailed in Part 1, numerous instances of apparent evil circulate and recur in the world. This occurs either due to the choices of sinful humans or as a result of decreed punishments.

The matter initially seems to contradict His will, blessed be He. Indeed, He desires only good and aims to bestow good upon His creations. The dominance of the wicked and the strengthening of evil and corruption desecrate His Blessed Name. However, those who understand His ways and delve deeply into these matters, realize that all these events are part of a complex chain leading to the complete rectification of creation, as outlined in Part 1. Ultimately, it becomes clear that the Creator truly directs everything, and His counsel to bestow goodness and perfection upon His creations prevails, as explained previously. Yet, according to the true nature of the situation, things must progress through these sequences, based on the principles of profound wisdom and true goodness. In the end, it will be evident that He alone, orchestrated all these events to achieve the ultimate good that we mentioned.

Furthermore, these complex sequences reveal the truth of His oneness. We have already explained that the general course of events in the world involves the Blessed Creator creating evil, prompting humans to eradicate it and establish good within themselves and the world. Numerous laws and significant principles underpin this process, ensuring its comprehensive development from all perspectives. There are many aspects to consider regarding the existence, actions, and dominance of evil in creation, as well as humanity's relationship with it. This includes our subjugation to evil, our efforts to overcome it, and our progress beyond its constraints. Similarly, we must consider the existence of good, its spread, and its strengthening in direct proportion to our conquest of evil.

The very existence, actions and dominance of evil stem from the Creator's decision to conceal His oneness, which is not fully apparent to all. The level of concealment directly correlates with the strength of evil's presence, as discussed in Part 1. Conversely, the complete eradication of evil, the establishment of creation in goodness, hinges on revealing the truth of His oneness. This is the essence of the verse "See now that I, I am He,"[49] and the statement "In order that you know and believe...before Me no God was formed nor shall there be after Me."[50] Thus, the final rectification of all creation depends on unveiling His oneness. He was, is, and will eternally be One and Unique. Although this is not fully apparent to all at present, it will be in the future, as stated, "On that day God will be one and His name will be one."[51]

Israel, having merited His true Torah, already acknowledges this truth and bears witness to it, which is a great privilege for us.

---

[49] Devarim. 32,39
[50] Is. 43,10
[51] Zach. 14,9

Divine providence is categorized into daytime and nightime providence, as elaborated in Part 3, Chapter 1. Every morning and evening, angelic arrangements and assignments are renewed according to the providential order. We, the children of Israel, are duty-bound to testify to the truth of His oneness in all its aspects: in existence, acknowledging that He alone necessarily exists, and all other existences stem from and depend on Him; in dominion, affirming that He alone, blessed be His Name, is the singular Ruler, and no actor acts without His permission and empowerment; and in providence, recognizing that despite the numerous, profound, and lofty causes, there is only One who causes everything to unfold according to His plan, ultimately achieving the true purpose, which is complete perfection. While this truth may not be fully revealed at present, it is the undeniable reality, and it will be universally acknowledged and understood in the end.

The matter of His kingship requires further discernment. The Blessed Creator is sovereign over all His creations. To elaborate, His Blessedness exists independently, not contingent upon anything else. He is inherently perfect, having no need for connections to any other entity, regardless of whether they are above or below Him. He does not depend on any cause, not as an effect relies on its cause, nor as a composite relies on its elements. In this regard, He is referred to as Elokim, signifying His self-existent nature.
However, His role changes when He chooses to create. All created beings rely on Him for their existence and all aspects of their being. In this context, He is the Master of all, as everything

originates from Him, belongs to Him, and is governed by His will. Despite this, out of His benevolence and care, He chooses to humble Himself, so to speak, and engage with His creations, even though they are fundamentally unrelated to Him. He wishes to be seen as a king to a nation, positioning Himself as their leader and deriving glory from them as a king does from his subjects, as highlighted by the verse, "With the greatness of a nation, a king is glorified."[52]

In this role, He is perceived as our leader, drawing glory from our existence and service. Consequently, we are obligated to serve Him and obey His commands as a nation would its king. This obligation extends to recognizing Him daily, upholding His sovereignty over us, and submitting to His decrees as servants would to their king. This act of submission is termed accepting the yoke of the kingdom of Heaven, encapsulated in the first verse of the Shema. It involves acknowledging His supreme rule over all creations, celestial and terrestrial, and willingly placing ourselves under His dominion.

The implications of recognizing His oneness and accepting His sovereignty are profound for the entirety of creation. The structure of creation and its entities are designed in such a way that when His kingship is acknowledged, and all beings recognize Him, prosperity and tranquility prevail, blessings flourish, and peace increases across creation. Conversely, when beings rebel, refusing to submit to and acknowledge His sovereignty, goodness diminishes, darkness ensues, and evil

---

[52] Prov. 14,28

prevails. These dynamics ripple through all levels of creation, influencing both active and passive entities.

While His kingship remains constant, regardless of our recognition, our actions as lower beings undeniably impact the manifestation of His rule. If conditions necessitate His revelation in kingship, it results in immense good and tranquility for creation, an increase in divine enlightenment and purity, and the subjugation of evil forces. Should this not be the case, He conceals His presence, allowing evil forces to dominate.

This dynamic applies universally, wherever relevant. When Israel diligently strengthens their commitment to His kingship daily, both internally and externally, it prompts divine revelation in the world. Evil is suppressed beneath the forces of good, resulting in an outpouring of blessings. By affirming His oneness, we invoke a reciprocal response, with the Holy One, blessed be He, elevating His oneness and amplifying the processes of rectification in creation. This aligns with the ultimate rectification mentioned earlier, guiding creation with mercy and overlooking transgressions. Consequently, enlightenment, holiness, brightness, and sanctity are bestowed upon creation, proportional to what is deemed appropriate.

Another great rectification joins this, embodied in the praise 'Blessed be the name of the glory of His kingdom forever,' spoken subsequently. As we have established, His influences and illuminations draw through varied mechanisms, all rooted in and dependent on His oneness and true perfection. Through this entire system, creations undergo various incarnations, aiming ultimately at attaining perfection through His true perfection. The supernal wisdom has decreed that creations can only draw or attain this perfection through these mechanisms, after all their incarnations. When activity and dominion unify with His oneness, everything becomes dependent on Him. All influences reveal themselves as mere extensions of the oneness, serving as pathways for creations to reach Him. Since the intent of the first verse is to establish dependence on the oneness, all influences hinge on this, returning to the concept of true perfection we discussed earlier.

This results in His Name spreading among creations, His sanctity binding powerfully to them. He governs them, perpetually drawing them towards Him. They find themselves dependent on Him, perfected through His perfection, achieving this true state ultimately, after all their incarnations. In this state, His will, may He be blessed, finds fulfillment; His honor amplifies, achieving the essential glorification He receives from His creations. However, this completion currently exists only in the spiritual realm. There, entities are pure and holy; His Name rests upon them, associating powerfully with them. They constantly follow Him, magnifying His honor. In contrast, the lower realms have yet to achieve full perfection. Evil still mingles within them; they are not yet purified, resulting in His honor not being properly magnified through them.

The angels, residing in their rectified state, express this praise of 'Blessed be the name of the glory of His kingdom forever.'

The lower realms, however, cannot join in this praise, as they are not yet worthy. The Name does not rest upon them adequately, nor is the glory properly magnified through them. An exception was our forefather Jacob, peace be upon him. At the time of his passing, surrounded by his holy sons, free from defect, they were crowned with His oneness. They declared 'Shema Yisrael etc.,' to which the elder responded 'Blessed be the name of the glory of His kingdom forever.' Thus, it became apparent that from our perspective, we are generally unworthy of this, except for what was granted to us through our forefather Jacob. Therefore, we utter this phrase, but in a subdued manner, except on Yom Kippur. On that day, Israel ascends to the level of angels, as elaborated upon elsewhere.

The other paragraphs serve to complete the message encapsulated in three key principles: accepting His dominion, fostering love for Him, and embracing the duty to follow His commandments, along with remembering the exodus from Egypt. In the first paragraph, one should aim to fortify their love for the Divine, embracing all its facets « Loving with all your heart, soul, and might ».[53] This involves inviting the Divine's sanctity into our lives, accepting His dominion over us, and ensuring these legacy passes onto our children and all future generations, as highlighted in the phrase "You shall teach it to your children."[54] It is about holistic betterment, improving our state of being whether at home, in transit, etc., and by

---

[53] Devarim. 6,5
[54] Devarim. 6,7

extension, enhancing the state of our households, as implied in "You shall inscribe them etc."[55]

Upon accepting the yoke of His commandments with the verse "It will be if you hearken,"[56] one proceeds to recall the exodus from Egypt in the passage about Tzitzit. This event marked Israel's redemption, their separation from the intermingling with other nations. Until then, the physicality of all mankind was marred by prevailing darkness and impurity. The exodus was a purifying process for Israel, preparing their bodies for Torah and divine service, symbolized by the commandments to eliminate leaven and consume Matzah. Bread, a staple for human sustenance, metaphorically represents the ideal human state. The leavening process, while natural and enhancing the bread's digestibility and taste, parallels the human condition, acknowledging the necessity of evil inclination and physical tendencies. However, for a limited period, Israel was to abstain from leaven, subsisting on Matzah to weaken their base inclinations, shifting their focus to spirituality. This practice, though temporary, was crucial, as a perpetual state of such abstinence is neither feasible nor desired in this world. The festival of Pesach is central to this concept, with other commandments of the first night intricately tied to the details of that redemption.

One more correction is included in reading all these sections, which is, to correct every aspect of a person's faculties in the

---

[55] Devarim. 6,9
[56] Devarim. 11,13

light of His Oneness, and likewise to correct in him every detail of creation. For behold, a person's faculties altogether are 248, corresponding to his 248 limbs. And similarly, the aspects of creation according to their fixities are also 248, corresponding to a person's 248 limbs. Both of these need to be corrected in the light of His Oneness, and this is accomplished through the 248 words in the Shema.

Our Sages composed for this purpose the blessings of the Shema recital. For each day, the entire existence is renewed before Him, may He be blessed, in two aspects: one - in the aspect of existence and continuity, as the flow renews itself each day to exist and endure in its existence; and second - that all the days of the 6000 years. They are all fixed and stand before Him, may He be blessed, in the aspect of illuminations and existential influences and states, that are always necessary for the desired cycle to be completed and arrive at perfection. Thus, each day is literally a new aspect, and in that aspect the entirety of existence renews itself every day, as it says, "Who renews Creation each day, constantly." On this principle these blessings and praises were instituted, on all the creations, which renew themselves day by day.

All these creations divide into two categories: the first is all the creations of the lower and upper worlds, and the second is humankind, specifically Israel, who are truly the human species. In this order the first blessing was composed, praising all the creations and their ministers, which are the creations below and the angels above, each one in its order. Included in this is the matter of day and night and the luminaries that rule over them. The second blessing praises the matter of Israel and the love with which He loved them and brought them near to His service. All these matters are included in their true ways in these blessings. Afterwards is the Shema, and afterwards another blessing was composed on all the great miracles that the Master of the worlds performed for us, focusing on the Exodus from Egypt in its details, arranged according to its true mysteries and all its aspects.

The essence of this is in the morning, as mentioned, that this is when existence renews itself. But at night an additional matter is added for all creations, according to the nature of night, which is only like the completion and perfection of the matters of the day. In this aspect as well, the blessings of the evening Shema were arranged similar to the morning Shema blessings, but more concisely, as it is only a summary repetition according to what renews in the order of providence, following what was renewed in the day. They added the blessing about the restfulness of night and sleep in all its aspects, which is the blessing of "Who spreads over us the shelter of peace".

Chapter 5 - Prayer

The subject of prayer is rooted in the decree of the Supernal Wisdom. For beings to receive divine flow, they must actively seek closeness and divine favor. The intensity of their pursuit determines the extent of the divine flow they receive. Absence of effort results in the absence of flow. The Creator, master of all worlds, desires the continual growth of His creation's goodness. He established a daily service for them to draw success and blessing, tailored to their worldly needs.

Yet, there's a deeper aspect to consider. The Creator endowed humans with knowledge and understanding to navigate their world intelligently. He tasked them with managing their needs, based on two principles: firstly, the honor and significance of humans, granted this wisdom to act rightly; and secondly, their engagement with worldly affairs, a necessary but non-sacred part of their existence. This involvement, though seemingly a downgrade, is essential for eventual elevation, as elaborated in Part 1. However, excessive entanglement in worldly matters distances them from divine light, leading to spiritual darkness. The remedy is first seeking proximity to the Divine, casting all needs and reliance upon Him. This initial act ensures that subsequent human efforts don't lead to over-absorption in materialism, as the prior divine reliance tempers the descent.

Concerning the approach to prayer and the customary three steps back post-prayer, the Divine, in His kindness, allowed humans a means to transcend their inherent distance from divine light. He permitted them to stand before Him, call upon His name, and momentarily rise above their natural lowliness. This act of prayer signifies closeness to the Divine, not to be interrupted. The concluding steps back symbolize a return to one's regular state, necessary for daily life.

Our Sages, blessed be their memory, outlined specific conditions for prayer to fulfill its intent, including the approach and the drawing down of influence. They crafted the prayers and blessings, detailing all laws and aspects.

The foregoing discussion on the Shema and prayer aligns with the intended purpose of these commandments. Our Sages also structured the prayer order to substitute for the now-absent sacrificial service, aligning with the daily renewal and temporal laws. This will be explored further in the next chapter, God willing.

Chapter 6 - The Order of Prayers

The Supreme Wisdom has ordained that night should be a time when the forces of impurity have dominion, spreading through all their chariots, and their branches roam the world. During this time, people gather in their homes, lying in their beds, sleeping and resting until morning. In the morning, the dominion and spread of those forces and all their branches are removed, and people rise and go out to their work until evening.

This is as King David, peace be upon him, explained, "You make darkness and it is night," and also, "The sun rises...man goes out to his work..."[57] Yet, all these matters in all their parameters and measurements are rooted in the foundations of providence, according to the aspects of the influences bestowed on created beings at all their levels, as explained in Part 1. It is generally said that night is a time of dominion for these forces, but in truth, this is only in the first half of the night. At midnight, an influence of illumination and will is bestowed before Him, may He be blessed, upon all the worlds. Dominion is removed from the evil forces, their branches are banished from settled places. The illumination of day begins to arouse, until day breaks and the fitting influence is drawn and all existence renews within it.

____

[57] Psalms. 104,20-23

However, the matter of the dominion these forces have at night and their banishment by day, this is something decreed in the nature of the world and its order, aside from dominion and subjugation which comes upon them through human deed. The Supreme Wisdom ordained that for the existence of true good and evil, which follows from the deeds of those with free choice, the world in its natural state must be liable to domination by evil within it, in a way that thus there will be potential for the spread of this evil in some parts of it, just as there is potential for its absence in them.

For this to be so, the Supreme Wisdom decreed it fitting that in time itself there should be one part which gives it dominion and spread intrinsically, as preparation for what may be given it by human deeds. There should be another part that removes dominion from it, as preparation for what human deeds may cause for it. Thus, there are two powerful existences, light and darkness, deriving from the illumination and concealment that we explained in Part 1. They were given a portion in time, namely day and night, and after them follow the dominion of the forces of impurity that we mentioned and their banishment, all as preparation for the consequences of deeds, as stated.

When this dominion is given to these evil forces and they spread through the world, the world's darkness increases and intensifies. A person, too, lying in his bed, has the spread of the roaming impurity extend onto him, to the degree it is allotted, corresponding to its connection to the human body because of its physicality and evil inclination within it. Additionally, it was already prepared in the order of providence that when a person sleeps, the higher parts of his soul withdraw from him, as explained in Part 2, and he tastes an aspect of death to a degree, which our Sages, may their memory be blessed, wrote, "Sleep is one-sixtieth of death." Thus, the darkness in his body then intensifies, with the absence of the light of the soul that purifies it.

Therefore, a greater gateway is found there for impurity to rest upon him, which is the matter of an "evil spirit" that our Sages explained rests on the hands. However, its resting specifically on the hands and not another place is because this is the measure and boundary that the Supreme Wisdom delimited for it - what could rest upon a person, which is fitting according to his state in the world, no less and no more. The Supreme Wisdom prepared for a person what he should engage in during the morning, to rise up from the low state of night, to purify from the impurity, and similarly, the entire world will rise up from its lowness and be illuminated from the darkness that darkened it. This entire matter is included in the remedies established for the time of rising, from deeds and speech, as will be explained, God willing.

The initial act is the purification of the hands. These hands, having become impure as the evil spirit rested upon them, require banishment of this impurity. The Creator, blessed be He, has decreed that this banishment be achieved through proper washing, in accordance with the teachings of our Sages. Through this act, not only the hands but the entire body of the person is purified, just as it had become wholly impure due to the resting of the evil spirit upon them. This act of purification extends beyond the individual; it is also a rectification for the entire universe. It serves to cleanse the universal impurity of night and to emerge from its encompassing darkness. In conjunction with this act of purification, there is the practice of the individual cleansing their body by relieving themselves, thereby becoming entirely purified and ready to approach their Creator.

Following this, two additional deeds are performed, which are among the 613 commandments. These deeds are integrally connected with the remedies of prayer and are essential in completing the daily service. These are the commandments of tzitzit and tefillin. The specific details of each of these commandments will be elaborated upon first, followed by an explanation of their roles within the daily service remedies previously mentioned.

The matter of tzitzit concerns the desire of the Master of worlds for Israel to rectify themselves in all aspects through holy practices. Consequently, He issued commandments applicable to every time and situation, enabling them to achieve rectification through these practices. This includes the garments a person wears. In order for these garments to be sanctified, He commanded the placement of Tzitzit on them, thereby rendering them holy. Moreover, this commandment encompasses a profound significance: it marks a person as belonging to God, akin to a servant marked by their master.

This act signifies the acceptance and subjugation under His yoke. It empowers a person to contribute to the rectification of the entire universe, as detailed in Part 1. In doing so, one partakes in the Creator's work, striving to maintain the universe He created in its intended state. This achievement is realized through human deeds and actions, as prescribed by the Torah and its commandments.

The crux of this entire service hinges on one principle: humanity's role as servants of the Creator, entrusted with the monumental task of rectifying the universe, a responsibility placed squarely in their hands. Consequently, the success of this endeavor is contingent upon human actions, which yield corresponding outcomes.

The weight of this responsibility, akin to the yoke a master places upon a servant, is exemplified through specific elements outlined by the Master of worlds, including the symbolic representation of tzitzit. Beyond being an eternal commandment, our Sages have integrated Tzitzit as an integral aspect of prayer, manifesting in the practice of wrapping oneself in a Talit during prayer. This act reinforces the acceptance of His yoke, committing to the labor of world rectification – Tikun Olam.

However, the significance of Tefilin surpasses that of Tzitzit. The Creator bestowed upon Israel the privilege of drawing down a tangible extension of His holiness upon themselves, to be adorned with it. This endowment encompasses both their spiritual and physical realms, subjecting them to this profound light for extensive rectification. As the verse states, "All the peoples of the earth will see that the name of God is called upon you,"[58] this divine connection is dependent on the observance of this commandment with all its detailed laws. In humans, two primary organs - the brain and the heart - wield considerable influence over the soul.

The Creator's command involves the drawing down of divine light onto the brain first through the head Tefilin, thereby sanctifying both the brain and soul within. Subsequently, this light extends to the heart via the hand Tefilin, leading to its sanctification. Through this process, a person in their entirety is enveloped in this divine holiness, achieving a state of profound sanctity. The intricate components of this commandment are crucial for achieving the desired comprehensive rectification, in alignment with the various facets of human existence.

On most days, the commandment is to adorn oneself with Tefilin. However, on holy days, which themselves symbolize a sign for Israel, this adornment is inherent, not requiring the additional act of wearing Tefilin. On such days, the level of spiritual adornment achieved inherently surpasses that which is attained through the effort of donning Tefilin on regular days. Nevertheless, every aspect of this practice, including the days when Tefilin is not worn, is meticulously determined by the Supreme Wisdom to align with what is most fitting.

____

[58] Devarim. 28,10

Following the wrapping with Tzitzit and adorning with Tefilin, the structure of prayers was established to effectuate the necessary rectification. The overarching goal of these prayers is to prepare the entire universe and all its worlds to receive and be receptive to the supernal influence, drawing it forth from the Divine. Prayer is broadly divided into four sections: the Offerings, Psalms, Shema and its blessings, and the Amidah Prayer, along with subsequent elements.

The offerings aim to purify the entire world, removing obstructions to the flow of supernal influence. The Psalms are intended to unveil the light of His countenance through our praises and glorification of His glory. This act of exaltation, as defined by the Creator, is embodied in the concept of "choosing songs of praise." The Shema and its blessings, already discussed, include the notion of the structured order of Creation, with beings descending level after level from potential to physical form.

The Supreme Wisdom decreed that for all created beings to receive divine influence, a hierarchical connection is required, starting from the lower levels to the higher and ascending further up to the highest potentials. These connections enable the flow of Divine influence, which then spreads appropriately through all levels of Creation, allowing them to be fixed in their designated roles. The blessings of the Shema are crafted around these mystical concepts, elevating the levels of Creation from the lower to the higher, culminating in a connection to the ultimate light, thereby drawing influence to all creations, as manifested in the Amidah Prayer.

It is important to recognize that the types of supernal influence, encompassing all varieties and specifics, are represented by three primary forms, symbolized in the three letters of the name Havayah. Their collective manifestation in the universe is indicated by the final Heh. Corresponding to these are three Divine attributes: great, mighty, and awesome. The appropriate channeling of these influences is attributed to the merits of the patriarchs Abraham, Isaac, and Yaacov.

The outspouring of these influences, derived from their collective synergy, is linked to the merit of King David, who connects with the patriarchs and completes the spiritual rectification of Israel. In alignment with these three forms of influence, the first three blessings of prayer were formulated.

They facilitate the general drawing down of the supernal influence, which is then detailed in the middle blessings, and finally solidified and grounded in the recipients through the gratitude expressed in the last three blessings. This process constitutes the comprehensive rectification accomplished through prayer.

On weekdays, this prayer structure is adhered to. However, on holy days, the Sages limited the burden to no more than seven blessings. These days, inherently holy and blessed, aid in the drawing down of influence. Therefore, it suffices for an individual to focus on the generality, represented by the seven blessings: the initial three corresponding to the three forms of influence and the final three in a similar vein. The central blessing pertains to the day's overarching holiness, enhancing its strength, illumination, and governance, thereby supporting and augmenting all specifics. Further elaboration on this will be provided later, God willing.

It is also essential to understand that the universe is broadly segmented into four worlds[59]: this world, encompassing both its higher and lower aspects, the celestial realm, - planets and stars, and the terrestrial realm, termed the lower world, collectively forming one world Asiah - Action. The World of Angels, Yetsirah — Formation and above it, the World of Creation - Beriah, the roots of creation as mentioned in Part 1, referred to as the World of the Souls. Above this tier lies the aggregate of His influences, the revelations of His light, from which all existences derive and upon which they depend, as elucidated in Part 3 Chapter 2.

By extension, this entire spectrum of influences can be termed one world, labeled the World of Emanation - Atsilut. This designation, however, is applied metaphorically, for reasons to be explained, distinguishing it from the preceding three worlds where the term applies more concretely. A 'world' is defined as a collection of diverse entities in a space, categorized in various ways and interacting with each other.

---

[59] Asiah, Yetsirah, Beriah, Atsilut

This definition applies accurately to both physical and spiritual entities. Thus, our world is termed a 'world' as it is a congregation of lower or celestial bodies in one space. Similarly, the World of Angels is termed so as it consists of many angels congregated as applicable to them. The World of the Creation is also a 'world' as it comprises numerous forces within their relevant space. In contrast, His influences are not a collection of diverse entities but rather various forms and types of His light's revelation, solely purposed for His creations and their unique influences.

However, since these influences are differentiated in terms of order and levels, fitting for their recipients through whom these distinctions, orders, and levels are established - as detailed in Part 3 Chapter 2 - this collective is termed a 'world', placed above the other three realms. This is because, hierarchically, the entire chain of creation ascends to this level: the physical realm leading to the angels, the angels to the higher realms, namely the Throne (world of Emanation) and its levels, and the Throne ascending to the revelation of the light of God, constituting the true origin of all.

The structure of prayer is established in accordance with this order – the three initial sections dedicated to rectifying the three worlds: this world, the World of Angels, and the World of Creation, represented respectively by the Offerings, Psalms and Shema blessings. Following these is the Standing Prayer - Amidah, correlating with the World of Emanation, to channel influences according to their respective aspects. Subsequent sections are designed to facilitate the flow of this influence through the worlds sequentially until culmination. These include: Sanctity of the Order, Song of the Levites, and There is None Like our God. The sequence concludes with Aleinu, intended to reaffirm His dominion over all worlds after their reception of blessings from Him.

Additional specific practices are incorporated to invoke mercy and enhance blessing. These include confession, the recitation of the 13 Attributes, and bowing down. Confession serves to silence accusers, preventing them from hindering the acceptance of one's prayer. Invoking the 13 Attributes harnesses their power, prompting the Creator to adhere to His attribute of mercy, and, in His supreme loftiness, to overlook transgressions and pardon iniquity in the absence of merit. Bowing down signifies profound submission before Him, whose immense power can soften the attribute of justice, stirring great mercies and drawing abundant influence and relief. This framework constitutes the general structure upon which prayer is founded. Within this framework, numerous details are interwoven, each with its specific place and purpose, including Psalms and other verses, each contributing to the overall tapestry of prayer.

In the divine order of providence, the day is divided into two parts: morning, and afternoon. The night, is similarly divided in two. During each of these segments, illumination and influence must be drawn to the worlds, corresponding to the specific aspect of that time. Prayers are thus instituted accordingly:

Shacharit and Mincha for the two parts of the day. In the morning, a time of renewed influence reflecting the day's aspect, the order of prayer is fully implemented to meet all needs. For the afternoon, succeeding the morning, only a certain level of effort is required to complete the day's spiritual tasks. At night, given its more dynamic nature compared to daytime, a more extensive order than Mincha is implemented, particularly the blessings of the Shema recital. However, this night-time order is shorter than the morning's, as the influence from the morning still prevails.

For the latter half of the night, no fixed order is set for everyone, to avoid overburdening the community. Instead, this period is left to the discretion of the devout, each engaging in prayer according to their understanding and fervor. The evening prayer, initially a voluntary practice, later became obligatory, further emphasizing the importance of the midnight rectification. While the three daily prayers were instituted by the patriarchs, making them incumbent upon all Israel, the additional midnight prayer, as exemplified by King David's practice of rising at midnight to give thanks, was not made obligatory for all, but rather remained a practice for the particularly devout, thus maintaining a distinction from the patriarchal level of commitment.

On holy days, an additional prayer, known as the Musaf, is added. This prayer corresponds to the extra offering unique to these days, reflecting the additional spiritual influence characteristic of these occasions. The Musaf prayer mirrors the elevated sanctity and thematic elements of the holy days, enhancing the regular prayers and adding a layer of solemnity and celebration. It acknowledges the distinct spiritual opportunities presented on these days, aligning the prayers with the day's unique holiness and spiritual potential.

The Musaf, like other prayers, is carefully crafted to resonate with the specific sanctity of each holy day, ensuring harmony between the prayers and the day's spiritual offerings. This comprehensive approach to prayer, encompassing both routine and special occasions, underscores a deep understanding of the intricate interplay between human actions, divine influence, and the cosmic order. The prayers, in their various forms and timings, act as a conduit connecting the earthly and the divine, guiding the faithful towards spiritual elevation and alignment with the divine will.

Chapter 7 - Periodic Worship

Temporary worship is what we are obligated to do at certain times. It includes observing the Sabbath and its holiness, observing the ninth of the Month (9 Av) and its affliction, observing the festivals, sanctifying the intermediate days of the festivals, refraining from leaven and eating Matzah in their proper times, sounding the Shofar, sitting in the Sukkah and taking the Lulav at their proper times, and observing Rosh Chodesh, Hanukkah and Purim. Now we will explain their concepts.

The general concept of the Sabbath is that, as we have already explained above, the matter of this world dictates that things within it are profane and not sacred. However, it was also necessary that on the other hand, some sanctity be granted to creations, so that darkness does not overly prevail in them. Indeed, the Supreme wisdom has measured all this with utmost precision, determining at what level the profane and at what level this additional sanctity should be, and set these limits appropriately in terms of quantity, quality, place, time and all the distinctions that must be examined in existence.

Moreover, in terms of time, the Creator arranged the matter of weekdays and holy days and within the holy days themselves, levels one above the other as appropriate. It has arranged that most days will be profane, and holy only to the extent necessary. However, it decreed that the days should all revolve in a fixed number, rotating in their entirety in a cycle, and this is the number of seven days. This is because in them the entire existence was created, and all its being is included in this number, and this number is what is appropriate to be called a complete measure, since it was all needed for the existence of all being, and more than this was not needed at all, for in it all being was completed.

However, this number will keep revolving and going and returning in its cycles until the end of all the six thousand years. Not only that, but the days of the entire world will also maintain this measure, that is, six thousand years and one thousand of rest. Afterwards, the existence will be renewed into another order as decreed by the Supreme wisdom. Since the end of the cycle will always be in sanctity, this elevates all the days greatly, that although most of them are profane and only one part out of seven is sacred, which is what is necessary for this world as we mentioned. On the other hand, by having this part be the end of the cycle and its seal, the entire cycle is rectified and elevated through this, until all the days of man are sanctified. This is a great gift that God gave to Israel, wanting them to be a holy nation, which was not given to the other nations at all, as this elevation is not fitting or intended for them.

Just as Israel achieves this spiritual elevation on this day, so too should their behavior befit it. However, the ways of the world, as we have explained above, is of the sort that binds a person to materialism. Therefore, one should sever this connection on the Sabbath, as one's affairs are elevated beyond the weekday concerns, and should hold oneself to the standard befitting this elevated state. Yet to completely detach from physicality and its affairs is impossible, for in this world one is bound by physical ties. But the Supreme wisdom has designated the degree to which one should sever from physicality and the degree to which one must remain within it. The levels from which one should detach, are the commandments and laws for all the labors that are prohibited on the Sabbath.

Aside from refraining in order not to diminish the holiness bestowed on this day, we are also commanded to honor this holiness through delighting in Shabbat, honoring its arrival and departure with Kiddush and Havdalah, and all its other details. All these are based on maintaining ourselves at the level appropriate for the holiness bestowed on us, cherishing this elevation, honoring the matter of its holiness which is a great closeness to God. Honoring and clinging to Him who gave us such a great gift.

The supernal wisdom further decreed additional holiness for Israel, giving them holy days aside from Shabbat, through which they would receive degrees of holiness below the level of Shabbat. Accordingly, we must detach from worldly affairs based on the degree of influence and illumination. Yom Kippur is the highest, then the festivals, the Intermediate days when some labors are forbidden, Rosh Chodesh, then Chanukah and Purim when no labor is forbidden, just thanksgiving on

Chanukah and joy on Purim. All according to the degree of influence and illumination on these days.

Aside from the graded levels of sanctity according to the holiness of each day, there are also specific matters unique to this particular time based on its concept. Their root is the order decreed by the Supernal wisdom that whenever the time recurs of a previous rectification and great illumination, a reflection of that original light shines once more, recreating that rectification in those who receive it.

Therefore, we are commanded to recall the exodus on Passover, since that was an exceedingly great rectification in which we were rectified. When that time recurs, a reflection of that original light shines, recreating that rectification in us. Similarly, Shavuot for the giving of Torah, and Sukkot for the Clouds of Glory, though it is not precisely the same time, the Torah established this festival for commemoration, as it says, "In Sukkot I housed you." Similarly for Chanukah and Purim.

This was also the concept of the fast days recorded in Megillat Taanit, which were nullified because Israel could not endure them, though they were exempted from commemorating them to stimulate their original lights. Now we will explain these commandments individually.

Chapter 8 - Time-Bound Commandments

The meaning of leaven and Matzah is that until the Exodus from Egypt, Israel was intermingled with the other nations, one nation among the nations. With their departure from Egypt, they were redeemed and separated. Until that time, the physical aspect of all human bodies was enveloped in the darkness and impurity which had overpowered them. With the Exodus, Israel was separated and purified to become fit for Torah and divine service.

For this purpose, they were instructed about the importance of nullifying leaven and eating matzah. Bread, when prepared for human consumption, symbolizes the desired state within a person. Leavening, which is bread's natural state enhancing digestion and taste, aligns with the proper norm for a person – the need for the evil inclination and physical desires. However, Israel had to refrain from leaven and eat matzah for a specific, measured time, minimizing their evil inclination and material desires. This strengthens their spiritual closeness. Constantly sustaining this state is impossible and not desirable in this world. Rather, it is appropriate to maintain this during the allotted time, helping them reach the level appropriate for them, this is the essence of Pessah. The other commandments of the first night are specific matters corresponding to the details of that redemption.

The significance of Sukkah and Lulav lies in the Clouds of Glory with which God surrounded Israel. These clouds provided not only physical shelter and protection but also brought great spiritual benefits. Just as these clouds isolated Israel, elevating them above the ground, they also imbued them with an illuminating aura, separating them from other nations and elevating them above the mundane world, making them supreme over all nations. This was initially to bring Israel to a supernal level suitable for them, and its impact continues in every generation. Each righteous Jew is surrounded by a holy aura, isolating them from others, elevating them, and making them supreme.

This is recreated on Sukkot through the Sukkah. God's light shines on Israel, instilling fear in their enemies, especially when taking the Lulav and its species, as the Scripture says, "All the nations of the earth shall see that God's Name is called upon and they shall fear you"[60]. If not for sins, this would be apparent to all. However, it will come to fruition in its time. The Lulav commandments, with their specific actions of waving and encircling, complete this – strengthening God's dominion over Israel, subduing their enemies, and leading them to choose servitude under Israel. This is the meaning behind 'Nations will bow to you' and similar scriptures. They will become subservient to Israel, seeking the divine aura resting on them. Their arrogance will be subdued, serving God through Israel. This is the purpose of every detail of the lulav.

---

[60] Devarim. 28,10

Commemorating Chanukah and Purim highlights the divine illumination present during these historical events and the spiritual rectifications achieved. Chanukah acknowledges the Kohanim's resilience against the Greeks, leading to a renewed commitment to Torah and its teachings, exemplified by the Menorah's rededication. Purim celebrates the Jewish people's salvation in Babylonia, highlighting their renewed acceptance of the Torah, as the sages emphasized: 'They re-accepted it in the days of Achashverosh.' The celebrations reflect the unique spiritual rectifications of each festival.

On Rosh Hashanah, the Shofar plays a pivotal role. It's the day when God judges the world, renewing existence for a new year. The divine court convenes, and every creature is judged according to celestial justice, as detailed in Part 2 of our discussion. Just as divine justice dictates that goodness is granted only to those who are deserving, there are actions that, when performed by man, ensure that he is treated with mercy and compassion, irrespective of strict adherence to the law. This is encapsulated in the sage's teaching: "One who is forgiving of others, they are forgiving of all his sins." Thus, the Shofar, when sounded with proper intent and coupled with sincere repentance, has the power to invoke divine mercy, overwhelming the forces of evil and nullifying the power of the accusers. The specifics of this ritual and its connection to divine mercy are rooted in the fundamental nature of divine guidance.

Yom Kippur is a divine gift, offering a day of accepted repentance and easy erasure of sins. The goal is to repair spiritual damage from sin dispel the darkness it brings, and restore the sinner to a state of holiness and divine proximity. The day's special illumination aids this process, but to receive it, one must adhere to the prescribed rituals of atonement, notably the afflictions that elevate one's spiritual state. The specific practices and their connections to spiritual rectification are tailored to the unique nature of this holy day.

The prophets established the practice of Torah reading as a significant spiritual rectification for Israel. This includes two primary practices: cyclical reading of the entire Torah scroll, and the reading of specific sections at specific times. The Torah, in its entirety, represents the divine wisdom bestowed upon us, and its verbalization draws forth divine illumination. To maintain a constant connection with this divine light, communal reading of the Torah in order has been instituted, supplementing the individual study that each person is encouraged to undertake privately. Additionally, reading specific sections at particular times harnesses the power of the Torah to enhance the spiritual illumination of those times. The details of these practices are intricately connected to the nature of the spiritual rectification they aim to achieve

Chapter 9 - Circumstantial Service and Blessings

Circumstantial works are the everyday events of human beings, in their food, their clothing, and all their earthly needs.

In general, all this is based on what we have already explained: every subject in all areas of the world, whether governed by law or chance, in whatever existence, has been founded and decreed with the aim of reaching the ultimate true purpose of creation that we have mentioned. All these details were necessary, each within its own limits.

The need for all these details and their forms stems from the different levels of reality and the influences exerted upon them. In all these areas, commandments were given to ensure that things stay on the side of good and not evil. When these actions are thus framed, what results from them is good and corrective. Otherwise, impurity and darkness spread, according to the nature of the subject in question.

It is on this model that our Sages instituted blessings on all subjects of the world and its pleasures. The root of this is the Blessing after the Meal, as ordained in the Torah.
Indeed, all subjects engraved in nature aim, at their level, for the ultimate goal, which is the fulfillment of the entire existence. However, man should always intend to serve his

Creator in his actions dictated by nature. Everything that results from these actions to help achieve this purpose will thus be considered as pertaining to divine service, in whatever way it may be.

Therefore, regardless of their level, these subjects should only be undertaken for this purpose, and not from material inclination. They must be kept within the limits set by the Divine Torah, to truly serve as aids towards the ultimate goal. Thus, the Torah has taught us that after enjoying our food, we must thank God and bring the matter back to its true objective: the fulfillment of His will, until His glory is magnified. This is the essence of the blessing after the meal, and of every blessing after a pleasure.

Our Sages also added to ordain blessings before the pleasure, to further elevate the act: even before using the world, one must mention the Divine Name, receive this good from Him, and have the intention that it is not just a material pleasure but something prepared by Him for the true good. Thus, in performing this act, one elevates oneself instead of the opposite.

Similarly, in the performance of commandments, our Sages instituted blessings, to thank God for His blessings and great rectifications. We are then further elevated, with divine assistance. For the more we awaken to Him, the more He helps us in return.

"Happy is he who trusts in the Lord."

The Books of the Ramchal

The Ramchal wrote more than eighty books on Kabbalah, ethics, morality, philosophy, and more. Most of his books have been lost and today we are only aware of these books

מסילת ישרים	סוד ה' ליראיו
דרך ה'	תקט"ו תפילות
מאמר העיקרים	תיקונים חדשים
דרך חכמה .	קיצור כוונות
דרך עץ החיים	עיקרי הדינים
דרך תבונות	אגרות רמח"ל
דעת תבונות	ירים משה
ספר הכללים	ספר השירים
קל"ח פתחי חכמה	שרשי המצוות
קנאת ה' צבאות	ספרי דקדוק ומליצה
אדיר במרום	לשון לימודים
משכני עליון	ספר ההגיון
מאמר הגאולה	ספר המליצה
זוהר תנינא	ספר הדקדוק
עשרה אורות	מחזות קודש:
פנות המרכבה	מעשה שמשון
האילן הקדוש	מגדל עוז או תומת ישרים.
מאמר הוויכוח	לישרים תהילה
חוקר ומקובל	בנין עולם
מלחמת משה	פתחי חכמה ודעת
רזין גניזין	

Description of Some Books of the Ramchal

Adir Bamarom

Adir Bamarom by the Ramchal is a commentary on the section Adrah Rabah of the Zohar. which is a seminal text in the study of Kabbalah. The Ramchal aims to clarify and elaborate on the Zohar's teachings. Each section builds upon the previous one, leading the reader to a more profound understanding of kabbalistic thought and concepts.

Derech Eitz Chaim

Derech Eitz Chaim (The Way of the Tree of Life) is a profound guide to Jewish meditation and prayer. It is not divided into chapters in a modern sense but is rather a continuous discourse divided into sections that deal with various aspects of spiritual practice and prayer. The text is aimed at guiding the reader towards achieving a closer communion with the Divine through a deeper understanding and practice of the mitzvot (commandments) and prayer, with a particular focus on the kavanot (mystical intentions).

Hokhmat HaEmet

"Hokhmat HaEmet" (The Wisdom of Truth) is a work about the exploration of Kabbalistic truth and delves into the Ramchal's understanding of divine wisdom as it pertains to the nature of God, creation, and the path to spiritual enlightenment. It also contains a series of discourses on various topics within Jewish mysticism and philosophy.

Messilat Yesharim

Messilat Yesharim - Way of the Justs by Rabbi Moshe Chaim Luzzatto - the Ramchal, is a classic work of Jewish ethical literature. Written in the 18th century. It is a practical guide to moral and spiritual growth, rooted in the Mussar tradition. It's structured around the steps one must climb to reach spiritual perfection.

Each chapter in "Messilat Yesharim" is designed to be a stepping stone, gradually leading the reader from fundamental concepts to more advanced stages of spiritual growth and moral excellence. This work is characterized by its clarity, practicality, and depth, offering guidance that is as relevant today as it was when it was written.

Klach Pitchei Chochmah

Klach Pitchei Chochmah - 138 Openings of Wisdom is a Kabbalistic text that is complex and dense, containing deep mystical insights into the nature of the divine and the universe. The text is not structured in a typical chapter format, but rather as individual entries or "openings" that explore various aspects of Kabbalistic wisdom. These openings are concise sections, each discussing different elements of the Sefirotic system, the structure of the divine realms, and the interplay between the physical and the spiritual.

Ma'amar HaGeulah

Ma'amar HaGeulah, or "Discourse on the Redemption," is a kabbalistic exposition on the themes of exile and redemption as they pertain to both individual spiritual states and the collective destiny of the Jewish people and the world, particularly those concerning the ultimate redemption or 'Geulah.'

Migdal Oz

Migdal Oz, which translates to "Strong Tower," is another one of the Ramchal's kabbalistic works. The title itself suggests a focus on strength and fortitude in the spiritual realm, likely drawing from Proverbs 18:10, "The name of the Lord is a strong tower; the righteous run into it and are safe." It contains a series of interconnected discussions or essays on various spiritual and mystical themes and also includes intricate discussions of divine emanations and the ways in which they interact with the world and humanity.

Kinat Hashem Tzevaot

Kinat Hashem Tzevaot - "The Zeal of the Lord of Hosts." This work discusses the passionate commitment of God to His purposes and plans, particularly as it relates to the defense of His honor and the fulfillment of His will through the history of Israel and the unfolding of the cosmos. And the divine zeal as it pertains to the rectification and purification of the world, leading to the final redemption.

Sod Hageulah

Sod Hageulah - Secrets of Redemption is in line with Ramchal's kabbalistic philosophy, it likely explores the deeper spiritual dimensions of redemption (Geulah), both personal and collective. It blends profound kabbalistic insights with practical guidance, encouraging readers to live with an awareness of the redemptive process and to participate in it through spiritual growth and ethical conduct. Each section would build upon the last, forming a comprehensive picture of the Ramchal's vision of

Sefer HaKavanot

Sefer HaKavanot, which translates to "The Book of Intentions," is a mystical manual that delves into the kavanot, or specific mystical intentions and meditations, one should have during the performance of Jewish prayers and commandments (mitzvot). The Ramchal, in this text, elaborates on the profound spiritual roots of Jewish practices and how each act can be a conduit for drawing down divine influences and rectifying the various spiritual realms.

Zohar Tinyana

Zohar Tinyana, -The Second Zohar, is an extension of the themes found in the classic Zohar, written in a similar style. The Ramchal uses the form of a mystical commentary to delve deeper into the secrets of the Torah, expanding upon the spiritual and ethical teachings contained within the original Zohar.

Ma'amar HaVikuach

Ma'amar HaVikuach - The Kabbalist and the Philosopher is a philosophical work by the Ramchal. This work is structured as a dialogue between a philosopher and a Kabbalist and is intended to defend the Kabbalistic worldview against philosophical criticisms.

The Ramchal uses this dialogue to reconcile the seemingly divergent paths of rational philosophy and mystical tradition, arguing that Kabbalah provides a deeper understanding of the world that complements rather than contradicts rational thought.

The philosopher in the dialogue represents the rationalist approach, seeking to understand the world through logic and observation. In contrast, the Kabbalist represents the mystical tradition, which includes esoteric knowledge and divine revelation as sources of truth.

Da'at Tevunot

Da'at Tevunot -The Wisdom of Consciouness is one of the major works of the Ramchal. The book is structured as a dialogue between the intellect and the soul, exploring the nature of divine wisdom and justice. It addresses profound questions about God's management of the world, the purpose of creation, the role of mankind, and the process of redemption.

Samples of books of the Ramchal translated by Rav Raphael Afilalo

The Way of the Justs - Mesilat Yesharim
The Wisdom of Consciousness – Daat Tevunot
The Kabbalist and the Philosopher - Meamar Havikuach

The Way of the Justs – Mesilat Yesharim

The Way of the Justs, is a classic work of Jewish ethical literature. Written in the 18th century. It is a practical guide to moral and spiritual growth, rooted in the Mussar tradition. It's structured around the steps one must climb to reach spiritual perfection.

Each chapter is designed to be a stepping stone, gradually leading the reader from fundamental concepts to more advanced stages of spiritual growth and moral excellence. This work is characterized by its clarity, practicality, and depth, offering guidance that is as relevant today as it was when it was written.

The author said: I did not compose this work to teach people what they do not know, but to remind them of what is already known and widely publicized among them. For you will not find in most of my words anything but matters that most people know and do not doubt at all. However, just as these matters are widely known and their truth is clear to all, forgetfulness of them is also very common and prevalent. Therefore, the benefit derived from this book does not come from reading it once, for it is possible that the reader will not find novel ideas in his mind after reading it that were not there before reading it, except a little. Rather, the benefit comes from reviewing it and persevering with it, for these matters that are naturally forgotten by people will be remembered, and one will take to heart one's duty which one overlooks.

If you consider the current state of most of the world, you will see that most people of quick understanding and sharp intellect apply most of their analysis and contemplation to the intricacies of different wisdoms and the depth of theoretical studies, each person according to his intellectual inclination and natural desire. Some exert great effort in studying the creation and nature, while others devote all of their theoretical analysis to astronomy and geometry, and others to crafts. Yet others delve further into the holy, that is, the study of the sacred Torah -- some in the give and take of halachic discussions, some in midrashim, and some in halachic rulings. But few belong to the category that establishes the study and analysis of matters of perfection in divine service, of love, fear, attachment, and all the other aspects of piety (chassidut).

This is not because these matters are not fundamental principles to them, for if you ask them, each one will say that this is the main principle. One cannot imagine a truly wise person for whom all these matters are not clear. Rather, the reason that they do not apply much analysis to it is due to the matters being so well-known and simple to them that they do not see a need to spend much time analyzing them. The study of these matters and the reading of books of this type is left only to those whose intellect is not so sharp and close to being coarse. You will see them diligent in all this and not budging from it, to the point that according to the practice prevalent in the world, when you see a pious individual, you cannot avoid suspecting him of being of coarse intellect.

However, the results of this practice are very detrimental for both the wise and the unwise, for it causes both to lack true piety, making it very rare to find in the world. It is lacking in the wise due to their limited analysis of it, and lacking in the unwise due to their limited grasp of it. As a result, most people imagine that piety depends on reciting many psalms, very long confessions, difficult fasts, and immersions in ice and snow -- all matters with which the intellect is not content and the mind is not at ease.

True piety, which is desirable and pleasant, is far from our conceptual image. It is a simple matter -- that which is not a person's obligation, he does not have in mind. Even though its basic principles are already fixed in the heart of every upright person, if he does not engage in them, he will see their details without recognizing them; he will encounter them without noticing them. See that matters of piety and matters of fear and love and purity of heart are not matters ingrained in a person such that he does not need means to acquire them. People do not find them on their own just as they find all of their natural functions like sleep and wakefulness, hunger and satiety, and all the other functions engraved in our nature. Rather, they certainly require means and strategies to acquire them, and there are also factors that detract from them and distance them from a person. There is no lack of ways to distance their detriments. If so, how can one not need to spend time analyzing this matter in order to know the truth of these matters, to know the way to acquire them and uphold them? From where will this wisdom come into a person's heart if he does not seek it?

Once the need for perfection in divine service and the obligation of its purity and cleanliness has been affirmed by every wise person -- for without these it is certainly not desired at all, but despised and abhorred, as "the L-rd searches all hearts and understands the inclination of all thoughts" (Chronicles 1:29:17) -- how will we respond on the day of rebuke if we were negligent in this analysis and abandoned a matter that is so incumbent upon us, as it is the essence of what the L-rd our G-d asks of us? Is it conceivable that our intellect would toil and labor in analyses that we are not obligated in, in give-and-takes from which we derive no benefit, and in laws that do not apply to us, while we leave the great duty that we owe to our Creator to habit and treat it as rote learned from others? If we did not contemplate and analyze what is true fear and its branches, how will we acquire it and how will we escape from the worldly vanity that causes us to forget it?

Will it not be forgotten and lost even though we know it is our duty? Love, likewise -- if we do not strive to instill it in our hearts with the force of all the means that bring us to it, how will we find it within us? From where will attachment and passion for Him, may He be blessed, and His Torah come into our souls if we do not pay heed to His greatness and His exaltedness, which give birth to this attachment in our hearts? How will our thoughts be purified if we do not strive to cleanse them of the blemishes that the physical nature inflicts upon them, along with all of the character traits that likewise require correction and straightening -- who will straighten them and who will correct them if we do not pay attention to them and do not examine the matter with great precision? Indeed, if we would analyze the matter with true analysis, we would find it in its true form and benefit ourselves, and we would teach it to others and benefit them as well.

This is as Solomon said: "If you seek it like silver and search for it as for treasures, then you will understand the fear of the L-rd" (Proverbs 2:4-5). He does not say, "Then you will understand philosophy, then you will understand astronomy, then you will understand medicine, then you will understand laws, then you will understand halachot," but rather, "Then you will understand the fear of the L-rd." You see that in order to understand fear, you must seek it like silver and search for it like treasures. Indeed, in what we have been taught by our forefathers and in what is well-known to every intelligent person in general terms -- will time be found for all other areas of analysis but not for this analysis? Why should a person not set aside times, at the very least, for this contemplation, if he is compelled to turn to other analyses or pursuits in the rest of his time?

The verse states, "Behold, the fear of the Lord is wisdom" (Job 28:28), and our Sages, may their memory be for a blessing, said (Shabbat 31b): "'Behold' means one, as in Greek they call 'one' hen." We see that fear is wisdom, and it alone is wisdom. Certainly, that which does not involve analysis is not called wisdom. But the truth is that great analysis is needed for all these matters -- to know them truthfully and not by imagination and false reasoning, and all the more so to acquire them and attain them.

One who contemplates them will see that piety does not depend on those matters that the foolish pietists imagine, but on matters of true perfection and great wisdom. This is what Moses our teacher, peace be upon him, teaches us when he says: "And now, Israel, what does the Lord your G-d ask of you, but to fear the Lord your G-d, to walk in all His ways, and to love Him, and to serve the Lord your G-d with all your heart and with all your soul, to keep the commandments of the Lord and His statutes?" (Deuteronomy 10:12). Here he encapsulated all the elements of the perfection of the service that is desirable to His blessed Name, which are: fear, walking in His ways, love, wholeness of heart, and observing all the commandments.

Fear is the awe of His exaltedness, may He be blessed, such that one fears Him as one would fear a great and awesome king, and is embarrassed before His greatness with regard to every movement that one is about to make, and certainly when speaking before Him in prayer or engaging in His Torah. Walking in His ways includes the entire matter of the rectitude of one's character traits and their correction, and this is what they, may their memory be for a blessing, explained: "Just as He is merciful, so should you be merciful" (Shabbat 133b), and the general principle of all this is that a person should conduct all of his character traits and all types of his actions according to integrity and morality. Our Sages, may their memory be for a blessing, encapsulated it as "All that brings glory to its Maker and glory to him from man" (Avot 2:1), meaning all that leads to the ultimate true good, meaning that its outcome is the reinforcement of the Torah and the betterment of the fellowship of states. Love is that love for Him, may He be blessed, should be instilled in a person's heart to the point that his soul is aroused to do what is pleasing before Him, just as one's heart is aroused to do what is pleasing to his father and mother, and he is distressed if this is lacking on his part or on the part of others, and he is zealous for this and rejoices greatly when he does something of this.

Wholeness of heart means that the service before Him, may He be blessed, should be with purity of intent, meaning for the sole purpose of serving Him and not for any other motive. Included in this is that one should be whole in service and not like one who hobbles between two opinions or like one who performs the commandments by rote, but that one's entire heart should be devoted to this. Observing all the commandments: As its literal meaning, that is, observing all the commandments with all their details and conditions.

Now, all these are general principles that require great explanation. I found that our Sages, may their memory be for a blessing, summarized these parts in a different order, more detailed and arranged according to the necessary progression in acquiring them properly. This is what they said in a baraita, cited in various places in the Talmud, one of them in the chapter "Before Their Festivals." These are their words: "From here Rabbi Pinchas ben Yair said: Torah leads to watchfulness, watchfulness leads to alacrity, alacrity leads to cleanliness, cleanliness leads to separation, separation leads to purity, purity leads to piety, piety leads to humility, humility leads to fear of sin, fear of sin leads to holiness, holiness leads to Divine inspiration, Divine inspiration leads to the resurrection of the dead."

Based on this baraita, I decided to compose this work to teach myself and remind others of the conditions for perfect service, according to their levels. I will explain regarding each one its matters and parts or details, the way to acquire it and what detracts from it, and the way to be vigilant against them. For I will read it, and so will all who find contentment in it, so that we may learn to fear the L-rd our G-d, and our duty before Him will not be forgotten by us. And that which the corporeality of nature strives to remove from our heart, the reading and contemplation will bring to our memory and arouse us to what we are commanded. May the L-rd be our support and guard our feet from being trapped, and may the request of the psalmist, beloved to his G-d, be fulfilled in us: "Teach me Your way, O Lord, that I may walk in Your truth; unite my heart to fear Your Name" (Psalms 86:11). Amen, may this be His will.

Explaining the general obligation of a person in his world

The foundation of piety and the root of complete service is for a person to clarify and verify what his duty is in his world and toward what he should place his outlook and aspiration in all that he toils for all the days of his life. What our Sages of blessed memory have taught us is that man was only created to delight in G-d and to bask in the radiance of His Presence, for this is the true delight and the greatest of all pleasures that can be found. The place of this delight is truly in the World to Come, for it was created with the preparation needed for this.

However, the means to arrive at this desired destination is this world. This is what they, of blessed memory, said (Avot 4:16): "This world is like a vestibule before the World to Come." The means that bring a person to this ultimate purpose are the mitzvot which G-d, blessed be His Name, has commanded us to perform. The place of performing the mitzvot is only in this world. Therefore, man was placed in this world first, so that through these means that are available to him here, he can reach the place that was prepared for him, which is the World to Come, to delight there in the goodness that he acquired through these means. This is what they said, of blessed memory

(Eruvin 22a): "Today is for doing them and tomorrow is for receiving reward."

When you contemplate the matter, you will see that true perfection is only attachment to Him, blessed be He, and this is what King David would say (Psalms 73:28): "But as for me, G-d's nearness is my good." And he says (ibid. 27:4): "One thing I ask of the L-rd, that I seek - that I may dwell in the House of the L-rd all the days of my life, etc." For only this is good, and all that people consider good besides this is vain and deceptive foolishness. However, when a person merits this goodness, it is fitting that he first toil and strive with exertion to acquire it. That is, he should strive to attach himself to Him, blessed be He, through the power of deeds that lead to this matter, and these are the mitzvot.

Now, the Holy One, Blessed be He, has placed man in a location where many things distance him from Him, blessed be He, and these are the material desires; if he is drawn after them, behold, he distances himself and moves away from the true good. Thus, he is truly placed amidst the fierce battle, for all matters of the world, whether for good or bad, are tests for man. Poverty on one hand and wealth on the other hand, as Solomon said (Proverbs 30:9): "Lest I become sated and deny and say, 'Who is the L-rd?', and lest I become impoverished and steal, etc." Tranquility on one hand and suffering on the other hand, until the battle is found before him and behind him. If he will be a man of valor and triumph in the war from all sides, he will be the perfect man who will merit to attach himself to his Creator and emerge from this vestibule to enter the palace to bask in the light of life. To the degree that he conquered his evil inclination and desires and distanced himself from what distances him from the good and strove to attach himself to Him, so will he attain Him and rejoice in Him.

If you delve further into the matter, you will see that the world was created for the use of man. However, it stands in great balance. For if man is drawn after the world and distances himself from his Creator, behold, he deteriorates and causes the world to deteriorate with him. But if he rules over himself and attaches himself to his Creator and uses the world only to assist him in the service of his Creator, he elevates himself and the world itself is elevated with him. For it is indeed a great elevation for all creatures to be of service to the perfect man who is sanctified with His sanctity, blessed be He. This is like the matter that our Sages, may their memory be for a blessing, said regarding the light that the Holy One, Blessed be He, stored away for the righteous, and these are their words (Chagiga 12a): "When the Holy One, Blessed be He, saw the light that He stored away for the righteous, He rejoiced, as it is stated (Proverbs 13:9): 'The light of the righteous will rejoice.'"

Regarding the stones that Yaakov took and placed around his head, they said (Chullin 91b): "Rebbi Yitzchak said: This teaches that they all gathered together into one place and each one said, 'Upon me the righteous one will rest his head.'"

Our Sages of blessed memory have indeed alerted us to this fundamental in the Midrash Kohelet (Rabba 7:13), where they said, these are their words: "'See the work of G-d, etc.' (Kohelet 7:13). "When the Holy One, Blessed be He, created Adam the first man, He took him and led him round all the trees of the Garden of Eden and said to him: Behold My works, how beautiful and praiseworthy they are! All that I have created, I created for your sake. Pay attention that you do not corrupt and destroy My world."

In summary, man was not created for his situation in this world, but for his situation in the World to Come. However, his situation in this world is a means for his situation in the World to Come, which is the ultimate purpose. Therefore, you will find that the statements of our Sages, may their memory be for a blessing, are numerous and they all follow one style, likening this world to a place and time of preparation, and the World to Come to the place of rest and eating what is already prepared. This is what they said: "This world is similar to a vestibule" (Avot 4:16), as they said, of blessed memory: "Today is for doing them and tomorrow is for receiving reward" (Eruvin 22a). "One who toiled on Shabbat eve will eat on Shabbat" (Avodah Zara 3a). "This world is similar to dry land and the World to Come to the sea, etc." (Kohelet Rabba 1:15). There are many such statements along this line.

You can truly see that no intelligent person could believe that the purpose of man's creation is for his situation in this world. For what is man's life in this world, and who is truly happy and tranquil in this world? "The days of our years among them are seventy years, and if with might, eighty years; but their pride is toil and pain" (Psalms 90:10) - with many types of pain, illnesses, ailments and troubles, and after all this, death. Not one out of a thousand is found for whom the world grants many pleasures and true tranquility, and even he, if he lives to a hundred years, has already passed and is negated from the world.

Moreover, if the purpose of man's creation were for his situation in this world, there would be no need for instilling in him such an important and lofty soul that would be greater even than the angels themselves, all the more so since it finds no satisfaction in any worldly pleasures. This is what they taught us, of blessed memory, in Midrash Kohelet, these are their words (Kohelet Rabba 6:6): "'And also the soul will not be filled' - To what is the matter comparable? To a villager who married a princess. If he brings her everything in the world, it is worth nothing to her, for she is a princess. So too the soul - if you bring it all the delicacies of the world, they are nothing to it. Why? Because it comes from above."

Similarly, our Rabbis, may their memory be for a blessing, said (Avot 4:22): "Against your will you were created and against your will you were born." For the soul does not at all love this world; on the contrary, it despises it. If so, the Creator, blessed be He, certainly would not create a creation for a purpose that is against its nature and despised by it. Rather, man's creation is for his condition in the World to Come. Therefore, this soul was placed in him, for it is fitting for it to serve, and through it man can receive reward in its place and time, so that nothing despised will befall his soul in this world. On the contrary, it will be loved and cherished by it. This is simple.

Now that we know this, we immediately understand the severity of the mitzvot that are upon us and the preciousness of the service that is in our hands. For behold, these are the means that bring us to true perfection, without which it cannot be attained at all. However, it is known that the goal is not reached except through the power of assembling all the means that were found and that served to reach it. According to the power of the means and their utilization, so will be the goal born of them. Any slight difference found in the means, its outcome will certainly be discerned with clarity when the time of the goal born of the assembly of all of them arrives, as I wrote, and this is clear. From now on, it is certain that the precision with which one must be exacting regarding the mitzvot and service must be with the utmost precision, as weighers of gold and pearls are exacting due to their great value. For their outcome is born in true perfection and eternal preciousness, above which there is no greater preciousness.

We have thus learned that the main existence of man in this world is only to fulfill mitzvot, serve, and withstand trials. The pleasures of the world should not be for him except merely as an aid and assistance, so that he will have contentment and peace of mind in order to turn his heart to this service that is incumbent upon him. Indeed, it is fitting for him that his entire orientation should be only to the blessed Creator, and he should have no other purpose in any act he performs, small or large, except to draw close to Him, blessed be He, and to break down all the barriers that separate him from his Maker. These are all matters of materiality and what depends on them, until he is drawn after Him, blessed be He, literally like iron after a magnet. Whatever he can think of as a means for this closeness, he should pursue it and grasp it and not let go of it.

And whatever he can think of as a hindrance to this, he should flee from it as one flees from fire. As it is said (Psalms 63:9): "My soul cleaves after You; Your right hand upholds me." Since his coming to the world is only for this purpose, namely, to attain this closeness by rescuing his soul from all that prevents it and causes it to lose out, now that we know and have clarified for ourselves the truth of this principle, we must examine its details according to their levels, from the beginning of the matter to its end, as Rabbi Pinchas ben Yair arranged them in his statement that we already cited in our introduction. They are: watchfulness, alacrity, cleanliness, separation, purity, piety, humility, fear of sin, and holiness. Now we will explain them one by one with the help of Heaven.

The Wisdom of Consciousness – Daat Tevunot

To Understand the Fundamental Principles of Faith

Soul: My desire and will is to settle on some of the things about which it is said (Deuteronomy 4:39), "And you shall know this day and consider it in your heart, that the Lord, He is God," for these are among the fundamentals of our faith which every person is obligated to pursue, to the best of their ability.

Intellect: Where are you heading? The principles are thirteen - on which of them do you wish to contemplate?

Soul: All thirteen principles are validated to me without any doubt; but some are both verified and understood, while others are verified by faith but not clarified through understanding and knowledge.

Intellect: Which are verified to you, and which are clarified to you?

Soul: The existence, unity, eternity, incorporeality and immateriality of God, the creation of the world, prophecy, the prophecy of Moshe, and the Torah from heaven and its eternity - I believe and understand all these without need for further clarification. But providence, reward and punishment, the coming of the Messiah and resurrection of the dead - I believe due to religious obligation, but would like to have a reason to be at ease with them.

Intellect: What difficulties do you have with these matters?

Soul: The great causes overturning in the world that seem to show the opposite of providence, God forbid. Especially since reason cannot see the end and purpose of things, how God leads His creatures, and what is the ultimate aim; for the deeds of the blessed God have such latitude that no heart can contain them. I would like you to teach me a straight path to understand the uprightness of these matters, without turning right or left.

Intellect: There are very difficult and profound issues here, such as the righteous suffering and the wicked prospering, which have troubled even the greatest sages and prophets, including Moshe. They cannot be fully comprehended.

Soul: I will leave the incomprehensible details. But at least provide me with upright general principles, so I may have counsel and reason amidst the latitude of these matters. What my knowledge does not reach, I will accept is not for me to complete.

Intellect: It is certain that the Holy One, blessed be He, established His world on justice and upright, faithful conduct, as the faithful shepherd testified (Deuteronomy 32:4), "The Rock, His work is perfect, for all His ways are justice; a God of faithfulness and without iniquity, just and right is He."

Soul: The uprightness of this justice and depth of this perfect counsel is what I desire to hear explained clearly.

The Purpose of Man's Existence and Service

Intellect: First we must clarify the matter of human existence and the service incumbent upon man, to understand the desired purpose in all this.

Soul: This certainly requires much contemplation to understand clearly in all its parts.

Intellect: The first foundation on which the entire structure stands is that the supreme will wanted man to perfect himself and all creatures for his sake - this itself will be his merit and reward. His merit is that he engages in and labors to attain this perfection, enjoying the fruits of his own efforts. His reward is that he himself will be perfected and delight in goodness forever.

Soul: This foundation includes many angles. I await to hear what you will build upon it, so I may comprehensively discern what it includes. But first, is there a reason why the supreme will wanted this?

Intellect: The reason is simple, and depends on the answer to another question - why did the blessed Creator want to create creatures?

Soul: You answer a matter that is equal for both of us.

Intellect: What we can comprehend is that God, the ultimate good, wanted to create creatures in order to benefit them, for if there are no recipients of good, there is no beneficence. For the beneficence to be complete, He knew in His lofty wisdom that the recipients should receive it through their own efforts, becoming owners of that good without shame, unlike one who receives charity. On this they said (Jerusalem Talmud, Orlah 1:3), "He who eats that which is not his own is ashamed to look at his face."

Soul: The reason settles in my heart. Now complete your words.

Intellect: From this premise emerges a great root to contemplate - the matter of deficiency and its perfection. We need to know what the deficiency is, its consequences, the rectification by which creation is perfected, the way of doing this rectification, and its consequences.

Soul: But I think we first need to understand the perfection man will attain when he has completed his work and rested from his labor. Then we can understand in retrospect all that we have mentioned, for what man ultimately attains is what he initially lacked and needs to strive to acquire.

Intellect: You have spoken correctly. We can now understand perfection in general, not in detail, but this general knowledge will allow us to understand the deficiencies in detail, for every deficiency is the absence of that perfection.

Soul: Say what you have to say about this perfection.

Intellect: This perfection is simple from Scripture and reason; it is that man will cleave to God's holiness and enjoy the perception of His glory without any hindrance or obstruction. As it is written (Isaiah 58:14), "Then you shall delight in the Lord"; (Psalms 140:14), "The upright shall dwell in Your presence"; (Ibid. 16:11), "Fullness of joys in Your presence," and many others like these throughout the words of the prophets and writings, revealed to all nations. In the words of our Sages (Berachot 17a), "The World to Come has no eating or drinking etc., but the righteous sit with their crowns on their heads and delight in the radiance of the Divine Presence."

Reason also dictates this, for the soul is a portion of God above, and its desire is certainly to return and cleave to its source, as is the nature of every effect that yearns for its cause and has no rest until it attains this. But the nature of this cleaving and attainment we do not have the power to understand amidst our current deficiencies. From this we discern that our deficiencies are the distance and hindrance interposing between us and God, making it impossible to cleave to Him as we will after the hindrance passes. This is the deficiency we need to strive to remove from ourselves in order to acquire the perfection we mentioned.

Soul: The reason settles in my heart. Now complete your words.

Intellect: Before proceeding, we must clarify the existence of man and the service incumbent upon him, to understand the desired purpose in all this.

Soul: This matter certainly requires much contemplation to understand it clearly in all its parts.

Intellect: The foundation on which everything stands is that the supreme will wanted man to perfect himself and all that was created for his sake; this will be his merit and reward. His merit - because he is found to be engaged and laboring to attain this perfection; when he attains it - he will enjoy the fruit of his labor and his share of all his toil. His reward - for he will be the perfected one, delighting in goodness forever.

Soul: This foundation includes many facets. I am waiting to hear what you will build upon it, so I may discern in retrospect what is included. But first, is there a reason why the supreme will wanted this?

Intellect: The reason is simple; it depends on the answer to another question: why did the blessed Creator want to create creatures?

Soul: You answer a matter that is equal for both of us.

Intellect: What we can comprehend is that God, may He be blessed, is the ultimate good. It is the law of good to do good; this is what He wanted - to create creatures so that He could benefit them. For if there is no recipient of good, there is no beneficence. For the beneficence to be complete, He knew in His lofty wisdom that it is fitting for the recipients to receive it through their own effort, making them the owners of that good, not remaining with shame in receiving it, like one who receives charity. On this they said (Jerusalem Talmud, Orlah, Chapter 1, Halacha 3), "He who eats that which is not his own is ashamed to look at his face."

Soul: The reason settles in my heart. Now complete your words.

Intellect: From this premise, a great root emerges for us to contemplate: the matter of deficiency and its perfection. We need to know what deficiency is, its consequences, its rectification by which creation will be perfected, the way of doing this rectification, and its consequences.

Soul: I think we first need to understand the perfection that man will attain when he has completed his work and rested from his labor. Then we will understand in retrospect all that we have mentioned. The reason is simple and clear: what man will ultimately attain is what he lacked initially, and because he lacks it, he needs to strive and acquire it.

Intellect: You have spoken correctly. We can now understand perfection in general, not in detail, but by knowing it in general, we will understand the deficiencies in detail in retrospect, for every deficiency is the absence of that perfection.

Soul: Say what you have to say about this perfection.

Intellect: This perfection is simple from Scripture and reason; it is that man will cleave to His holiness, and enjoy the perception of His glory without any hindrance or separating force. As it is written, "Then you shall delight in the Lord"; "The upright shall abide in Your presence"; "In Your presence is fullness of joy," and many others like these, revealed in the words of the prophets and the writings. In the words of our Sages, of blessed memory, "In the World to Come, the righteous sit with their crowns on their heads and delight in the radiance of the Divine Presence."
A logical reason: the soul is a portion of God above, and its desire is to return and cleave to its source to comprehend it, as is the nature of every effect that yearns for its cause,

having no rest until it attains this. But what this cleaving and comprehension will be - we do not have the power to understand as long as we are in the midst of deficiencies. From this, we discern our deficiencies, for just as perfection is this cleaving, the deficiencies are all the distance and hindrance that interposes between us and Him, making it impossible to cleave to Him as we will after the hindrance passes. This is the deficiency we need to strive to remove to acquire the perfection we mentioned.
Here we need a very fundamental premise.

Soul: What is it?

Intellect: That God, blessed be He, was certainly able to create man and all creation with ultimate perfection; it would have been fitting for it to be so, for Him being perfect in all kinds of perfection - it is fitting that His deeds should be perfect in all perfection. But when His wisdom decreed to leave man to perfect himself, He created these creatures lacking perfection. This is as if He restrained His attribute of perfection and His great goodness from acting according to the law of His greatness in these creatures, but to make them in the disposition He wanted according to the purpose intended in His lofty thought. Here is included another knowledge, as they said, "Shaddai - that He said to His world 'enough'"; that the heavens were stretching and going until He rebuked them, as written in the Midrash. Certainly, He could have created more and greater creatures than He did; if He had wanted to create His creatures according to the proportion of the Creator, they would have had no measure, just as He and His ability have no measure. But He created them according to the proportion of the created, measuring in them the fitting disposition for them according to what was intended. In any case, He certainly restrained, as it were, His great and infinite ability, so that it would not act in His creatures like its proportion, but according to the proportion of these creatures that are acted upon by it.

Soul: All this is certainly necessary, for it is of the faith that God, may His name be blessed, is omnipotent in all ways; it is impossible to set any limit or measure to His ability. Everything we see that was created from Him in a specific and limited measure - it will not be according to His proportion, God forbid, but according to what His will decreed to act.

Intellect: Let us establish this principle, then proceed to another fundamental premise. This principle: the Master has certainly prevented Himself, as it were, meaning that He prevented His ability in creating His creatures, not making them according to His power, but according to what He wanted and intended for them; He created them lacking so that they themselves would complete themselves, their perfection being their reward in the merit of their efforts to attain it. All this only because He wanted to bestow a complete beneficence.

Soul: Now let us hear this premise that you mentioned.

Intellect: The first premise we need to understand is where man's power is found to perfect his deficiencies, since he was created deficient. We are now entering a very great and wide sea, for we will need many great propositions before coming to complete our subject. You need to be very patient, to understand the matters in proper order, for this is the way of wisdom - to acquire knowledge one after another, until in the end everything will come to light as one complete matter, for which all those premises were needed.

Soul: Speak your words in the proper order, I am listening with all the patience and resolve required.

Intellect: First, you need to know that even though we have said that the blessed Master wanted to give perception of the essence of His perfection to His creatures, it is certainly not the will to give them perception of all His perfection which has no end, limit, or boundary; but on the contrary, only a small edge of it He wanted to reveal to them, in which will be all their delight in attaining it, as we have explained. This is very simple and desirable, for it is impossible for a consequent and created being like us to comprehend all the perfection of the Creator as it is said, "Can you by searching find out God? Can you find out the Almighty unto perfection?" It is found that all that creatures can attain will certainly not be even like a drop from the great sea of the perfection of the Creator, may He be blessed.

Soul: This is simple to all wise of heart, as it has been said, (Psalms 106:2), "Who can express the mighty acts of the Lord," etc.

Intellect: Now, when we consider all the orders of His deeds, all the great deeds He has done since placing man upon the earth, all that He has promised us to do through His holy prophets, what becomes clear to us with absolute clarity is the intensity of His unity. We see that all the other attributes of His perfection which have no end are not clarified to us at all, for we do not have the power to comprehend them. For example, we know that He is wise, but we have not comprehended the end of His wisdom; we know that He knows, but we have not comprehended His knowledge. Therefore they said, (Prayer of Elijah, Tikunei Zohar, Second Introduction), "You are wise, but not with a known wisdom, You are understanding, but not with a known understanding." Since we cannot comprehend these attributes, it follows that we are prohibited from investigating them, for about all such things it is said (Chagigah 13a in the name of Ben Sira 3:21), "You shall not seek what is too wonderful for you, you shall not investigate what is concealed from you"; so they said, (Sefer Yetzirah, Chapter 1), "If your heart runs - return to the place."

But His unity, on the contrary, is revealed and clarified to us with complete clarity. It follows that not only is it clarified to us, but we are obligated to consider this knowledge, to implant it in our hearts with complete resolve without any doubt at all. This is what Moshe our teacher, peace be upon him, commanded us from the mouth of the Almighty (Deuteronomy 4:39), "Know therefore this day, and consider it in your heart, that the Lord He is God in heaven above, and upon the earth beneath; there is none else."

The supreme mouth testifies of Himself and informs that all that is gathered from all His great causes with which He overturns in His world, is the revelation of this complete unity; as it is said, (Deuteronomy 32:39), "See now that I, even I, am He, and there is no god with Me," this verse was said after He included the entire cycle of the wheel, which was destined and prepared to revolve in the world, all included in the words of the song of Ha'azinu, as the plain meaning of the verses proves.

He sealed the conclusion of His vision with this language, "See now that I, even I, am He," etc. In the words of the prophet Isaiah, it is clarified explicitly (Isaiah 43:10-11), "That you may know and believe Me, understand that I am He; before Me there was no God formed, neither shall any be after Me. I, even I, am the Lord, and beside Me there is no savior"; as it is written (Isaiah 44:6), "I am the first, I am the last, and beside Me there is no God"; as it is written (Isaiah 44:6-7, "That they may know from the rising of the sun, and from the west, that there is none beside Me; I am the Lord, and there is none else; I form the light, and create darkness; I make peace, and create evil; I am the Lord, that does all these things." "That they may know," "that you may know and understand" it is written, implying that He wants us to know with knowledge and understanding. The ultimate of all the success that He promises to Israel is the clarification of His unity to the eyes of all. This matter is mentioned countless times in the words of the prophets, peace be upon them (Isaiah 2:11), "And the Lord alone shall be exalted in that day"; Zechariah 14:9), "And the Lord shall be king... in that day shall the Lord be One, and His name one"; (Zephaniah 3:9), "For then will I turn to the peoples a pure language, that they may all call upon the name of the Lord, to serve Him with one consent." In the end, this is our testimony every day continually (Deuteronomy 6:4), "Hear, O Israel: The Lord our God, the Lord is one."

It is found that all that is truly clarified to us from the intensity of His infinite perfection is only His complete unity. When we look with a contemplative gaze at all the deeds that have been done under the heavens, we see one course that revolves and goes, its rest being only the revelation of this truth. Now we need to understand this unity, what is desired in it, as the verse commanded us, (Deuteronomy 4:39), "and consider it in your heart that the Lord He is God," etc., implying that it requires the resolve of the mind and proper counsel in this matter. I have already said, this is a great and wide sea, in which we have to sail to our heart's content.

The Kabbalist and the Philosopher - Meamar Havikuach

Philosopher: Peace be upon you, my brother! How good is your coming at this time, for I am in great need of you.

Kabbalist: How can a philosopher need a kabbalist? You have already let your thoughts roam all corners of creation and subjugated it under you with your decisive proofs. How can I be of use to you?

Philosopher: Excessive praise is nothing but mockery. Let us come to the matter at hand. I will speak to you with the integrity of my heart, as is the way of our friendship. I have read and heard some matters from your Kabbalah, and they seem quite strange to me, for they contradict my investigations entirely. However, since I saw many pious individuals who followed its ways, I said to myself that I would see what you have to say. Perhaps I will hear from you something that, if not compelling, will at least not be contradictory and foolish according to sound reason, as it currently appears to me, leaving me no choice but to reject it.

Kabbalist: I will do as you say and inform you of the truth as it was transmitted to us by those who know the truth. The entire benefit of this knowledge will be that you receive from me another piece of knowledge: that you know that all a person can grasp through his philosophical inquiry is considered as nothing compared to what he can grasp through the true Kabbalah. Regarding this, the wise one said: "For the Lord gives wisdom, from His mouth come knowledge and understanding" (Proverbs 2:6). Now open your mouth wide, and I will fill it.

Philosopher: First, I wish to know from you about the sefirot that you mention - what are they? I would like to know this clearly, for I have heard such strange things about them that I had to restrain myself out of respect from crying out in the streets how astonished I was by them. I was nearly forced to say that they are nonsensical matters.

Kabbalist: Tell me what you heard about this.

Philosopher: I heard it said that they are one light that the Emanator, blessed be He, emanated from His primordial light, and that He, blessed be He, garbs Himself within them like a soul within a body.

Kabbalist: What else did you hear about this?

Philosopher: I heard that there is Atzilut, and there is Beriah, Yetzirah, and Asiyah. The difference between them is that Beriah, Yetzirah, and Asiyah are nothing but an illumination from this emanated light that we mentioned, and that it is divided into two parts. The inner part of it, meaning the soul, is called Divinity, while from the soul and below it is no longer called Divinity, but rather the "World of Separation." This applies to all three worlds.

Kabbalist: What do you say about this?

Philosopher: By the life of my soul, I do not even know how to arrange my difficulties due to their great quantity and quality, for this contradicts all reason and the truth of our faith.

Kabbalist: How so?

Four Difficulties Regarding the Sefirot of Atzilut

Philosopher: From now on, you will not escape one of these two options: Either you will say that they are Divinity, or not.

Kabbalist: But you already heard about this, that Atzilut is Divinity.

Philosopher: If it is Divinity, how can you conceive in your mind that Divinity can be derived from Divinity?

You said two things - that this contradicts all reason and our faith.

Philosopher: Indeed, regarding reason, it is as I said. For how can it be conceived that Divinity derives from Divinity? For God, meaning that Unique One who must exist to be the head of all creatures - since they are many, it is impossible for them to be conducted in an equal and fixed order except by a single head over them all. Therefore, we must understand that Unique One as the ultimate unity. How can we conceive of plurality, birth, and derivation of light within Him?

As for faith, tell me now, is this notion so far, God forbid, from the belief of the Christians, may their name be obliterated, who posited the Trinity, saying that He is three and He is one? For the One actually derives progeny from Himself, and yet it is all one. Furthermore, that which is renewed must not have existed prior to its renewal. If you say that the sefirot are new divinity, while the Infinite is ancient divinity, is this not exactly what is said about such things: "They chose new gods" (Judges 5:8)?

Additionally, how greatly do you stumble in faith, for we know that the Holy One, blessed be He, is absolutely simple, unaffected by any bodily contingencies. According to your words, there is no greater contingency than this - that His essence, blessed be He, should transform from non-existence to existence.

Kabbalist: You have already shaken the entire world with your words. Do you have any more such difficulties?
Philosopher: Indeed, I do. For now I spoke in general only about the matter of Atzilut. When we come to Beriah, Yetzirah, and Asiyah - they are exceedingly numerous. In truth, I have such strong questions and difficulties there that no mind of a wise and understanding person can bear them.

Kabbalist: Please state your words, and let me know what you have to say about this.

Difficulties Regarding the Sefirot of Beriah, Yetzirah, Asiyah

Philosopher: When you come to Beriah, Yetzirah, Asiyah, you make a continuum, and still call it Divinity. Afterward, you say that part of it is called Divinity, while part of it is not called by this name. Tell me, by your life, have you ever heard that Divinity could be divided to such an extent that half of it remains Divinity while half of it does not, but rather becomes a subservient slave to the first half? Believe me, faithful friend, these are not words of wisdom. It is impossible to bring such matters to the ears of an intelligent person, only to the simple-minded who believe everything.

However, there are two things I would like to know in any case: First, who involved us in this conflict? Second, what benefit emerges from this knowledge? Is the faith that the entire congregation of Israel believes - that the Creator is One, that He governs His world, that He gave His Torah to us, and that our Messiah will come - not good? What need do we have for all these matters of sefirot and worlds that breed nothing but confusion?

Kabbalist: Please complete your words.

Philosopher: I have one difficulty that encompasses all difficulties - that everything I have read or heard is astonishing from beginning to end. However, I think that if I would find at least one solid foundation upon which all these structures could be built, then perhaps the details would be comprehensible. But without that, why should I toil over the details when the entirety is difficult?

Can a Body Develop from Divinity?

However, I will not refrain from mentioning one strong difficulty I have with their words, which branches into two, but has one root:

I heard that you say that the sefirot developed level by level until this physical world came into being. This is an extremely difficult matter. What sense can there be to these words? How can that which is Divinity develop to the point of becoming one opaque body?

How Can We Understand the Emergence of the Other Side from Holiness?

The second, an even greater and more astounding difficulty, is what they say - that the Other Side emerged from the end of din (justice). Even more astonishing, they say that initially, good and evil were mixed together, and that is why the first worlds were destroyed, until the good was clarified by itself, which are the sefirot of holiness, and the evil by itself, which are the sefirot of the Other Side. To me, this matter seems almost like heresy, God forbid - to say that the Other Side was initially mixed into the sefirot, whether overtly or covertly. Say what you will, but they were one entity. How can one thing be clarified from it, with one part becoming the sefirot, which is Divinity, and the other part becoming the Other Side? I have no heart to accept these matters, and certainly not to utter them, for it seems to me that this leads to the heresy of two authorities, God forbid.

If the Sefirot are Divinity, How Can They Emanate from Divinity?

If you answer that the sefirot are light emanated from the Blessed Infinite One, and that is why such things are possible for them, this was already the first difficulty - how can one say that Divinity emanates from Divinity? If they are emanated from Him, they are outside of Him. Even if you say a hundred times that they are like a flame connected to a coal (Sefer Yetzirah 1:7), these are things said by mouth but are not accepted by the heart. For to say that something that is not essentially divine could still be divine is one of the impossibilities.

How Can We Understand Service Via the Sefirot?
Furthermore, according to your approach, all service is via the sefirot, and I see no permissibility for this. For we cannot escape the following: If they are not Divinity itself, then they must be able to be separate from Him and exist as vessels without light, like a body without a soul. Yet they are still described with the very attributes of Divinity - this is improper. For "the God of gods is the Lord" (Psalms 50:1), meaning the Holy One, blessed be He. According to your ways, it would mean Chesed, Gevurah, Tiferet. According to our faith, it is impossible to use these

names for anyone other than the Emanator, blessed be He. Rather, "You shall have no other gods before Me" (Exodus 20:3). If you answer that Divinity cleaves to them to such an extent that they are called by His name - such a thing should never be uttered, for you would be giving an opening to heretics, God forbid, and even worse.

In summary, these matters are very perplexing. Now, if you have the means to resolve them, if not entirely, then at least some of them, I would rejoice greatly.

Kabbalist: Until now, you have made yourself the witness, the judge, and the litigant. I, too, like you, will place you between Him and me as the adjudicator. Your reason will be the one I anticipate, as will you. But incline your ear and set aside your desire for just a moment, until you receive the true knowledge with a clear mind. Indeed, it requires resolution and conciliation.
Philosopher: Speak, and I shall listen.

Kabbalist: You are mistaken in every respect.

Philosopher: But I have heard many of your Kabbalists speak the very things I said.

Kabbalist: Their words need to be properly understood, not taken superficially.

Philosopher: Now let me hear a clear explanation from you.

This Wisdom Teaches the Unity of God and the Integrity of His Governance with Great Wisdom

Kabbalist: The foundation of this entire wisdom is the unity of the Emanator, blessed be He, that He is one in every way, without any change, plurality, or bodily contingency whatsoever.

Philosopher: The foundation is very good, if it can bear its structure.

Kabbalist: The entire matter of the wisdom of Kabbalah is nothing but an explanation of the attribute of His justice, blessed be He, the order of the laws of governance - how the Holy One, blessed be He, causes and governs all affairs of His world with great wisdom.

Philosopher: If this is what we would find in this wisdom, we would find something great. However, I do not see this wisdom proceeding along this path.

How Can We Understand Development in the Sefirot?

Kabbalist: Did I not tell you that you are mistaken in every respect?

Philosopher: I am stating what I gathered from the matters I read in your texts. I saw that you want to explain the chain of development - how the created being emerges from the Creator, as if the Creator, blessed be He, is the primary substance of the creations, developing from Him Himself. This primary substance gradually develops until it reaches the creations themselves. These are the sefirot and all that you expound upon regarding them. For you say that the Creator, blessed be He, placed His very name and was affected in one way until His own light was found to be affected and progressively developing until the lowest level was found. Now, if this matter could truly be stated, it would be very nice. For this development would certainly be the cause of all existences, and their variations would cause the variations in the world's affairs. Therefore, it would be good to know it, especially since the matter lends itself to attributing to it all the mitzvot and service, for it needs to be ordered according to its good nature. However, as I prefaced, if it could be said - for how can it be said that the light of the Creator, blessed be He, is affected or develops? You yourself have already admitted that contingencies do not apply to the Emanator, blessed be He.

Kabbalist: I acknowledge all this, and on the contrary, this is the foundation of my entire structure - that the Emanator, blessed be He, is not subject to any bodily contingency. But I said that you are mistaken in every respect, and I repeat it. It is impossible to say in any way that His light, blessed be He, is itself affected and develops to the extent that the Creator becomes a creation. Have you never heard that creation is something from nothing? If so, how can development and affectedness be spoken of?

Philosopher: Yes, your words have added water, now see to it that you add flour.

Understanding This Wisdom is Knowing His Governance, Blessed Be He

Kabbalist: But you will see that it is impossible for great sages to err in this, such as those from whom the Kabbalah flows to us. However, I will demonstrate to you that you did not understand anything of what you read. Do you know how to explain these levels mentioned in the sefirot, and all their variations mentioned at all times, what their benefit is in creation? How action and deed will result from them below? But inform me of the details, not generalities. If you know this, you can say that you understood what you read. If not, you will certainly say that you read what you did not understand.

Philosopher: Yes, in general I tell you that they are all matters needed to bring about the development of the world, and that through their differences in their states, they differentiate the affairs of the world. But in particular, I do not know what they are - not the qav (line) or the reshimu (impression), not Adam Kadmon, nor his worlds, the tikunim (rectifications) of the partzufim (visages) and their garments and intervals - all these are numerous. These are things I have read but do not know their nature. I only see great difficulties in them.

Kabbalist: If so, you do not know. I will start you on one path so you may see what you had not considered in these matters.

Philosopher: Speak.

Infinite and Sefirot - What He Can Will and What He Willed

Kabbalist: The Emanator, blessed be He, is certainly the Master of will, according to what He willed and wills. Now we can speak of Him in two aspects: in terms of His essence and in terms of His will. Do you admit this or not?

Philosopher: Certainly, we can speak about any subject in terms of each aspect of it independently. For example, when speaking about a person's affairs, the person is called the subject of the discussions, meaning the qualities being discussed about him are called the aspect or aspects of him. We can discuss an aspect of the person - that he is learned, charitable, or wise. Each of these is an independent aspect that we can discuss regarding each subject on its own.

Kabbalist: Regarding the essence of the Emanator, blessed be He, we are forbidden to speak of it, and we do not even need to delve into it at all. For it suffices us to know of His existence. When we know that He is the ultimate perfection, that He is omnipotent - we know what we need to know in this matter. Beyond this, we are already forbidden to even speak. Therefore, we will no longer speak of His essence, only of His will, for this is closer to us and is permissible, as we are not touching upon His essence at all.

Philosopher: It is good to speak of His will. But what can you say? His will has no end, His thought has no limit. What can you investigate regarding that which has no bounds or finitude?

Kabbalist: This is precisely what I wanted to elicit from you, that you admit that there is no end to His will and thought. From now on, you will not be able to flee from me concerning what I wish to impart to you. Please tell me, you certainly believe in reward and punishment, for it is one of the fundamentals of faith. But tell me: There are deeds in the world for which the Holy One, blessed be He, desires to benefit their doers, and there are those for which He desires to punish.

There is a time when He elevates and a time when He lowers; a time when He impoverishes and a time when He enriches. If so, in His will there is certainly a will of beneficence, a will of harm, a will of lowering, and a will of elevating. All this is certainly in order, for there is an order to the governance. If so, we can certainly discuss all of this, as we are not touching upon His essence, blessed be He, at all. In summary, these are the attributes of His will that we can certainly investigate and know.